SAMS
Teach Yourself
LINUX®

John Ray

in 10 Minutes

SAMS

A Division of Macmillan Computer Publishing
201 West 103rd St., Indianapolis, Indiana, 46290 USA

SAMS TEACH YOURSELF LINUX® IN 10 MINUTES

Copyright ©1999 by Sams® Publishing

International Standard Book Number: 0-672-31524-6

Library of Congress Catalog Card Number: 98-88374

Printed in the United States of America

First Printing: February, 1999

01   00   99   4

TRADEMARKS

WARNING AND DISCLAIMER

EXECUTIVE EDITOR
Grace Buechlein

DEVELOPMENT EDITOR
Laura Bulcher

MANAGING EDITOR
Brice Gosnell

PROJECT EDITOR
Natalie Harris

COPY EDITOR
Pamela Woolf

INDEXER
Kevin Kent

PROOFREADER
Benjamin Berg

TECHNICAL EDITORS
Rosanne S. Groves
Eric Richardson

INTERIOR DESIGN
Gary Adair

COVER DESIGN
Aren Howell

LAYOUT TECHNICIANS
Brandon Allen
Stacey DeRome
Tim Osborn
Staci Somers

TABLE OF CONTENTS

PART VII   ADVANCED TOPICS

PART VIII   APPENDIX

ABOUT THE AUTHOR

John Ray is an award-winning Web application developer and systems administrator for The Ohio State University. He holds a computer engineering degree from OSU and oversees network operations for one of its colleges. There, he implemented a campus-wide database for maintaining TCP/IP information for a variety of machines. He has also created a beginning-level programming language known as Weaver, which is used in OSU's Extension News database, as well as in several other high-end applications. For the past five years, John has used Linux exclusively for his programming efforts, and has championed its use for projects outside the University. He provides customized Linux- and UNIX-based TCP/IP programming solutions to businesses nationwide. You can reach him at: jray@poisontooth.co

DEDICATION

To my parents, my dog (for being so patient), and the ever-present Kiwi.

ACKNOWLEDGMENTS

I'd like to thank everyone who worked tirelessly to bring this project to fruition. Laura Bulcher, the development editor, for understanding what I was trying to say. Grace Buechlein, the executive editor, for managing to get everything organized within an impossibly short period of time. Anne Groves, technical editor, for an insightful and friendly tech edit! Lastly, my brother Will, whose collaborative efforts made it all possible. I hope that the book is as much fun to read as it was to write.

TELL US WHAT YOU THINK!

As the reader of this book, *you* are our most important critic and commentator. We value your opinion and want to know what we're doing right, what we could do better, what areas you'd like to see us publish in, and any other words of wisdom you're willing to pass our way.

As the executive editor for the Operating Systems team at Macmillan Computer Publishing, I welcome your comments. You can fax, email, or write me directly to let me know what you did or didn't like about this book—as well as what we can do to make our books stronger.

Please note that I cannot help you with technical problems related to the topic of this book, and that due to the high volume of mail I receive, I might not be able to reply to every message.

When you write, please be sure to include this book's title and author as well as your name and phone or fax number. I will carefully review your comments and share them with the author and editors who worked on the book.

Fax: 317.581.4663

Email: opsys@mcp.com

Mail: Executive Editor
            Operating Systems
            Macmillan Computer Publishing
            201 West 103rd Street
            Indianapolis, IN 46290 USA

INTRODUCTION

So You Want to Learn Linux

For years UNIX has been widely regarded as *the* network operating system. It provides the backbone for most of the Internet services that you are probably familiar with. As the Internet (and networks in general) has become more commonplace, the need for network operating systems has risen. The problem, however, is that while traditional versions of UNIX provide the facilities that people need, they generally come at a very high cost. Enter Linux!

Linux is (as you probably know!) a UNIX work-alike. It was developed by Linus Torvalds, and has continued development under his guidance. There are thousands of people worldwide who contribute to the Linux development effort. What makes this different from other operating systems is that these people work on Linux because they want to, not because it's their job and not because it's expected of them. The result is an operating system that is a labor of love—and it's entirely *free*.

Linux is distributed under the GNU Public License, which requires that its source code be free. Wait a second, aren't there companies selling Linux? Yes, there are many. These companies produce distributions of Linux that have extra features added, and include printed documentation. Even so, these commercial distributions are usually available as a completely free download (without documentation and support).

Besides being free, with its UNIX underpinnings, Linux is also a very powerful operating system. It offers protected memory, pre-emptive multi-tasking, and a full multi-user environment. You can use it to serve files, Web sites, and email—pretty much anything that you want. Unlike other server operating systems, Linux has very minimal system requirements and can run on hardware that has been delegated to the scrap heap. Furthermore, it operates on a wide range of different systems. Instead of a proprietary system for each kind of computer, Linux has been adapted for many different kinds of CPUs—from the Alpha to Intel Pentiums and IBM/Motorola PowerPCs. This means that you can run the same system on your Mac that you run on your Dell or Gateway...kind of nifty isn't it?

How to Use This Book

Linux can be a bit scary to many people. The power of the operating system lies in the command line. UNIX, and thus Linux, can appear cryptic to the beginner. That's where this book comes in. *Sams Teach Yourself Linux in 10 Minutes* introduces you to basic Linux commands in a way that is informative and easy to understand. By the time you finish this book, you will be comfortable with the command line and have the knowledge to find any other information you might need through Linux's extensive built-in help system. In addition, you'll learn about the KDE user interface, an elegant and high-powered point-and-click operating environment that is quickly becoming the desktop standard for Linux.

You can loosely divide this book into various sections. The first five lessons familiarize you with the Linux environment and navigate the Linux file system. The next group of lessons help you to learn file utilities, and the two groups of lessons after that give you the basics on working with the shell and customizing your environment. The final two sections help you learn to communicate with the outside world and give you a look at some of Linux's more advanced topics. I've also included an appendix with some guidance on selecting the Linux distribution that's right for you.

It is my hope that this book teaches you the skills you need to unleash the power behind one of the world's fastest growing operating systems: Linux.

Conventions Used in This Book

This book uses the following conventions:

- Information you type appears in **bold monospace** type.

- Screen output is shown in monospace.

- Menus and menu options, keys you press, and names of buttons and other screen components you might interact with appear in bolded blue type.

- The Return key is synonymous with the Enter key.

In addition, this book uses the following sidebars to identify helpful information:

 Tips lead you to shortcuts and solutions that can clear up confusion or save you time.

 Cautions help you avoid common pitfalls.

 Plain English explains new terms and definitions.

LESSON 1
GETTING STARTED

In this lesson, you'll learn how to log in to and out of your computer, the basics behind operating your Linux machine, and some background information on Linux functions.

A LITTLE BACKGROUND

Over the years, the UNIX operating system has gained the reputation of intimidating and scaring away many people. It has traditionally lived on fairly expensive machines in corporations and large organizations.

Linux has begun to change that landscape! It is an operating system that was born out of a computer science student's quest for something that looked and acted like the UNIX operating system but that was personal computer-friendly. Linux allows personal computers to work alongside expensive UNIX systems because it is essentially a re-implementation of the UNIX operating system from scratch.

A growing interest in Linux has spurred the development of utilities to make the user's life easier, and has aided in the push of Linux and other UNIX systems from the server room onto the desktop.

THE LOGIN PROCESS

The first thing you'll notice when you sit down in front of your Linux computer is that you need to log in before you can use it. Linux is a multi-user operating system, which means that multiple users can have their own accounts, programs, and settings stored separately on the same machine. If you're used to Windows 95/98/NT, this might sound similar to the concept of different users under Windows, and in some ways, it is. Windows 95/98 do not protect the user's files from other people; they simply hide the files. Furthermore, Windows 95/98 do not allow multiple users to run programs simultaneously; Linux does.

Ownership and Permissions

Linux has the concept of *ownership* and *permissions*. Files are owned by individual users, and permissions control who may view, edit, or run files on the system. Luckily, there is little need for a casual user to worry about ownership. If there is a need to share files with other users on the system, you'll want to take a look at Lesson 19, "Permissions." After you've logged in to your computer, all files that are created during that session will automatically be owned by your account.

Multi-user

Besides controlling and tracking who owns what, Linux also allows multiple users to access the system simultaneously. This is a drastic change from the desktop environment offered by traditional desktop operating systems. While you're working on a spreadsheet, a coworker might be running a series of calculations for an engineering project. Many different processes can be run on a single computer by potentially hundreds of different users. Lesson 11, "Processes," explains the concept of processes and how to manage them.

The Login Prompt

In order to log in to your computer, you need to supply a username and a password. You should have received these from your administrator, or you can choose one during the Linux software installation. After entering your information, Linux loads the appropriate configuration for your account and you are ready to start using the system. You'll find the screen that is displayed when you enter your username and password varies from system to system, depending on the configuration. There are two categories that you might encounter: a graphical login screen or a text-based screen.

 Watching Your P's and Q's   Linux is case-sensitive. Usernames, passwords, and directory names are all affected. For example, if you choose a password *HAPPY1*, it is not the same as *happy1*, or even *HAPPy1*. If you know you're typing your password correctly, but you still can't log in, check your Caps Lock button!

TEXT-BASED LOGIN

The text-based screen varies based on the Linux distribution you are using. The Caldera OpenLinux prompt, for example, looks like this:

```
Caldera OpenLinux(TM)
Version 1.3
Copyright 1996-1998 Caldera Systems, Inc.

login:
password:
```

At the login prompt, type your username and press Return or Enter. The password prompt appears immediately afterward. When typing your password, the data won't show onscreen in order to protect your account from prying eyes. If you successfully type both your username and password, you will reach a shell prompt and can begin issuing commands to the system. Don't worry if you don't know what to do next, you'll learn how to do something productive shortly!

 Oops! Don't worry if you make a mistake logging in. The system will log the failed attempt to a security file. In the default configuration, Linux gives you another chance to log in. There's no need to panic if you don't get it right the first time; everyone makes mistakes.

GRAPHICAL LOGIN

Instead of a text prompt, your machine might be configured with something a bit snazzier—a graphical screen where you can type your login information. This works exactly the same as the text-based system, but it immediately launches you into the X Window environment. If you work exclusively in X Windows, you might want to ask your administrator to install KDM or XDM, which provide graphical login services.

THE LOGOUT PROCESS

Now that you know how to log in to your system, let's take a brief look at how to log out and why it's important. You already know that your

computer can have multiple people using it simultaneously and that it can
have files owned by many different people. The login process identifies
you to the system, and lets you control the computer using your username; the logout process reverses this. It closes any files that you might
have open and shuts down any programs that you might have left running.
If you remain logged in constantly, you could be exposing the system to
security risks, or the processes you have left running might slow down the
computer for other users. It's always best to log out of your computer
when you're finished using it.

An important word of caution here: You should never turn your computer
off without running through the correct shutdown procedure. Pressing
Control+Alt+Del makes your machine run through an appropriate shutdown. It's best to do this from a login prompt so you don't lose any files
you're working on. Lesson 20, "Privileged Commands," demonstrates
other methods of shutting down your system.

LOGGING OUT FROM A TEXT-BASED SESSION

If you are not running a graphical session (there are no windows on
your screen), the only command you need to log out is, not surprisingly,
logout.

In order to log out from a command prompt, type

```
>logout
```

The system will immediately return to the login prompt. That's it. You've
successfully logged out of the computer.

LOGGING OUT FROM A KDE SESSION

If you logged in to the system through the KDE (K Desktop Environment)
graphical interface, you can point and click your way out of the system as
well. You'll learn more about the KDE system in Lesson 3, "The
Graphical User Interface." To log out

1. Click the **K** symbol to bring up the main KDE menu.

2. Select **Logout** from the menu

3. You will be prompted that KDE is ready to close your session.
   Click the **Logout** button to complete the process.

THE UNIX AND LINUX COMMAND PROMPT

You're probably wondering what use Linux is going to be to you if all you can do is log in and out. Patience! Linux can be a bit overwhelming if approached too quickly. The power of UNIX, and thus Linux, comes from the wealth of built-in utilities and the way that processes can be combined to perform tasks that would require customized programming on other operating systems. For example, suppose you're running a Web server on your Linux computer and you want to count the number of accesses from a machine named kiwi. If you're a programmer, it wouldn't be too difficult to write a program to do this, but you don't need to! Instead, you could just enter a command such as this one:

```
> grep "kiwi" /var/log/httpd/access.log ¦ wc -l
```

This counts the number of lines that contain kiwi in the Web server log file. Obviously you shouldn't know this yet, but you will by the end of this book. When you are typing commands into Linux, you are typing them into what is known as a *shell*. For all the old DOS users out there, a shell is equivalent to COMMAND.COM. If you remember the days of DOS, you probably also remember different DOS shells that added capabilities to your computer. UNIX has a wide variety of shells that you can use, each offering a different set of capabilities. Besides just giving the user a place to run commands, shells also provide a scripting language, much like a DOS batch file, but far more capable. Programs written using a shell are called *shell scripts*.

LOTS AND LOTS OF SHELLS

There are numerous shells available for Linux. Most people try the different shells and choose one that they like. If you don't plan on programming the shell, you'll probably never need to change your shell. Lesson 15, "User Utilities," discusses the techniques you can use to switch to a different shell. Here is a quick overview of just a few of the different shells that are available, and the benefits they offer.

- sh—This is *the* shell. It is available on any UNIX distribution that you might use, and it offers a simple scripting syntax. Most

people use sh only when they are writing programs that must
run on absolutely any UNIX machine.

- csh—The c shell. (Yes, it's pronounced sea shell.) The csh takes
  its name from the C programming language. The scripting environment that is offered by csh is similar to the C language, and
  offers enough flexibility to write lengthy customized scripts that
  run on most UNIX machines.

- bash—Bash is a modern shell that has received most of its attention from the Linux community, and is included as the default
  shell on most Linux machines. Bash offers the same capabilities
  of csh, but it offers advanced features for the user as well as the
  programmer. Bash includes command and filename completion
  and an easily accessible command history that is persistent
  across different login sessions.

There are far more shells available, but these three will probably make up
the bulk of any that you encounter. Don't worry if you sit down in front of
a computer that is running a different shell—you can still operate the
computer using the knowledge you'll gain in this book. You might experience some differences in the scripting architecture, but you're not going to
be lost.

SHELL COMMAND SYNTAX

Using a shell is as simple as typing the command you want to use and
pressing **Enter**. There are a few rules, however, that might help if you are
having trouble getting a command to work.

- Commands are case-sensitive, and are usually lowercase. Unlike
  Windows, you cannot mix cases and still have a function work;
  you must type the command exactly as it is stored on the system.

- Frequently, the current directory isn't included in your PATH
  environment variable. Your path includes the directories of all
  the commands that you can access by typing just the command's
  name (you'll find out how to modify this in Lesson 16,
  "Modifying the User Environment"). Because the current directory isn't necessarily included, you might be in a directory that

holds a program called *parachute* but you'll find that you can't run the program by typing **parachute**. In order to run the command, tell the system that the parachute command is in the same directory you are by preceding it with **./**. Thus, parachute could be run by typing **./parachute** from inside its directory.

 What's with the . and /? These characters represent the current directory (.) and the directory separator (/). Used together, ./ is essentially the path to the directory that you are currently in.

- There are special symbols, commands, and the like, that might leave your shell in a state that seems unusable. This generally means that you've started some sort of process that is expecting input from you. There are three control characters that might help you regain control of your commands. To type one of these control characters, hold down the control key while pressing the corresponding letter:

- Ctrl+d—Tells the computer that you are finished sending input to a command. This is useful if you've accidentally started a program and can't get out.

- Ctrl+c—The UNIX "break" character. This usually kills any program that is currently running, and then returns you to a command prompt.

- Ctrl+z—This suspends the current process you were running and returns you to a command prompt. Logging out kills the suspended command.

Don't be afraid to try the commands discussed in this book and explore the system to find more. You'll be amazed at what can be done with a little bit of typing.

SUMMARY

This lesson taught you a few very important skills that you will need to begin using your Linux computer effectively. Although most of the concepts introduced are relatively simple, they are important in understanding how and why Linux operates the way it does.

* **Login**—Logging in to Linux allows the system to identify you as a user and apply the appropriate ownership to files you create and modify. Each user has his or her own environment and can run programs simultaneously with other users.

* **Logout**—Logging out of the computer closes open files and ends processes that are owned by the current user. You should always log out of the system when you are finished using it.

* **Command line**—The UNIX command line allows you to create complex functions by stringing together a variety of built-in commands. What requires specialized software on other systems can usually be accomplished using built-in UNIX utilities.

* **Shells**—There are many different types of shells that you can use. Depending on your needs as a programmer and a user, you will need to evaluate the shell features you find necessary and choose appropriately.

* **Using the command line**—Commands can be typed directly into a shell, as you would expect. Keep in mind that commands are usually lowercase, and you might need to specify a path to the command if it is not included in your PATH environment variable.

LESSON 2

DOCUMENTATION AND FINDING HELP

This lesson provides several methods of retrieving information about the built-in commands and capabilities of Linux.

If you've poked around your Linux system a bit, you've probably noticed that there are literally thousands of different files and applications on your computer. You might find this to be a bit overwhelming at first, but the diversity and extensive capabilities of the operating system are part of its main attraction. If there is something you want to do, you can bet that Linux has a utility or combination of utilities that can help you get the job done. The biggest question on your mind is probably "How do I use this stuff?"

LINUX MANUAL PAGES

The Linux manual, or *man*, pages are the quickest and easiest source for information on how to use the commands on your system. They provide information on what programs do, how to use them, and other related utilities that you might be interested in checking out. If you're a programmer, man pages can also provide useful programming information.

man

To display a *manual page*, use the man command. In its simplest form, you type **man** followed by the command you want to look up. Because man pages change as software is updated, you might notice differences between man pages on different versions of Linux.

For example, to look up the man page for the date command, you would type

`>man date`

```
DATE(1)
DATE(1)

NAME
    date - print or set the system date and time

SYNOPSIS
    date  [-u] [-d datestr] [-s datestr] [—utc] [—universal]
    [—date=datestr]   [—set=datestr]   [—help]   [—version]
    [+FORMAT] [MMDDhhmm[[CC]YY][.ss]]

DESCRIPTION
    This  manual page documents the GNU version of date.  date
    with no arguments prints the current time and date (in the
    format  of  the `%c' directive described below).  If given
    an argument that starts with a `+', it prints the  current
    time  and  date  in  a format controlled by that argument,
    which has the same format as the format string  passed  to
    the `strftime' function.
    ...
```

 How do I Read the Rest? When you see an ... on your screen, that means there's more text to be read. The man pages won't scroll automatically, so you'll need to push the **Spacebar** to see additional text, and press q to quit the page and return to the command line.

This is only a tiny subset of the information that is returned via the man command, but enough to get the picture. You'll soon find that using man pages to find out about everything that is available on your system is going to take a bit of time. To speed things up, you can view a summary description of a command by using one of the four following: **man -f**, **man -k**, **whatis**, or **apropos**, followed by the name of the command you'd like to explore. Each of these functions will return similar results, but there are two different ways the search is performed.

man VARIATIONS, apropos, whatis

If you know the command you'd like to look up, use **man -f**, or **whatis** followed by the command name.

For example, to print a summary for the date command

```
>man -f date
date (1)                - print or set the system date and time
END
```

A short description of what date does is returned. You'll need to press **q** to return to the command line.

If you're not quite sure what you're looking for, **man -f** and **whatis** will search the description of each available command for matching keywords. If you experience any errors while running these commands, it might be because the whatis database has been removed from your system or has not been created. You'll need to contact your system administrator and ask her or him to use makewhatis to generate the database files necessary to use whatis. Because this is a function that affects protected areas of the system, it is not available to most users.

Now try running **whatis** on the **time** command. This should turn up several relevant entries.

```
>whatis time

time (2)              - get time in seconds
time (n)              - Time the execution of a script
Time::Local (3)       - efficiently compute time from local
➥ and GMT time
Time::gmtime (3)      - by-name interface to Perl's built-in
➥ gmtime() function
Time::localtime (3)   - by-name interface to Perl's built-in
➥ localtime() function
Time::tm (3)          - internal object used by Time::gmtime
➥ and Time::localtime
END
```

You can see that the time keyword has turned up six different entries in the whatis database. To return to the command prompt, you'll need to press **q**.

What do the Extra Letters and Numbers Mean? You notice that some commands are followed by a numeral or letter. This is the section number for that command. For instance, time is followed by both n and 2. This means that there are two separate uses for the time command. To learn information about each of the variations, use **man** followed by the section number or letter and the command. For example, **man n time** or **man 2 time.**

Lastly, if you're entirely unsure of what you want and a keyword search does not return anything useful, try the **apropos** or **man -k** command. This searches the descriptions much like whatis, but also displays partial matches to the string you specify.

Try running **apropos** on **time** and compare your results with the results from the similar whatis time command.

```
>apropos time

clock (3)          - Determine processor time
clock (n)          - Obtain and manipulate time
convdate (1)       - convert time/date strings and numbers
date (1)           - print or set the system date and time
difftime (3)       - calculate time difference
ftime (3)          - return date and time
ftpshut (8)        - close down the ftp servers at a given time
kbdrate (8)        - reset the keyboard repeat rate and delay
time
ldconfig (8)       - determine run-time link bindings
metamail (1)       - infrastructure for mailcap-based
↪multimedia mail handling
nanosleep (2)      - pause execution for a specified time
nwfstime (1)       - Display / Set a NetWare server's date
↪and time
parsedate (3)      - convert time and date string to number
...
```

This command actually turned up over 70 matches on my system, far more than whatis time displayed. Try to be as specific as possible when you use apropos or man -k or you might find yourself spending a great

deal of time wading through extraneous information. Don't forget, the ...
means there's more information to be accessed by pressing the **Spacebar**.
As before, pressing **q** returns you to the command prompt.

BUILT-IN HELP

Many of the Linux commands have a built-in help that isn't as verbose as
the man pages, and it can be brought up in a jiffy. If you find that you're
constantly using the man pages to find the options that are available for a
specific command, you might want to see if it has its own help summary
page. If you've spent much time using the compression or archiving utilities, you'll know what I mean. For many commands --**help** will provide
the information you need. In some cases, it might be as simple as --**h**. If
the first one doesn't work, try again. It's possible that built-in help is not
available, so don't be surprised if you run into cases where this doesn't
work as you had hoped.

To view the built-in help for the date command, you would type

```
>date --help

Usage: date [OPTION]... [+FORMAT]
   or: date [OPTION] [MMDDhhmm[[CC]YY][.ss]]
Display the current time in the given FORMAT, or set the
➥system date.

  -d, --date=STRING          display time described by STRING,
➥not `now'
  -f, --file=DATEFILE        like —date once for each line
➥of DATEFILE
  -r, --reference=FILE       display the last modification time
➥of FILE
  -R, --rfc-822              output RFC-822 compliant date
➥string
  -s, --set=STRING           set time described by STRING
  -u, --utc, —universal  print or set Coordinated Universal
➥Time
      --help                 display this help and exit
      --version              output version information and
➥exit
  ...
```

Although not as descriptive as the man pages, the information is useful
and to the point.

Depending on the resources that are available, your system administrator might have chosen to forgo the installation of man pages on your Linux system. The amount of disk space used by the manual pages is not trivial, and in these cases, you'll learn to appreciate the built-in help feature provided by many applications.

ADDITIONAL DOCUMENTATION

Linux distributions often come with a documentation directory filled with valuable information. Looking through the /usr/doc directory structure can reveal information that isn't found anywhere else.

PROGRAM SPECIFIC

Documentation for specific programs is often installed off of the /usr/doc directory. To get a look at what is installed on your system, type **cd /usr/doc** then **ls** to display what is available. These commands are fully explained in Lesson 4, "The File System." For now, just be aware that **cd /usr/doc** moves you to the /usr/doc directory, and **ls** lists the files in that directory. This is an area of the system that you should feel free to poke around. The information varies depending on the program itself. You might find information of the software's authors, Web pages, and so on—whatever the programmers decided to include. For example, the files containing information available for the at command on my system can be seen here (my at documentation is in the directory /usr/doc/at-3.1.7):

```
>ls /usr/doc/at-3.1.7/

ChangeLog  Copyright  Problems  README   timespec
```

You can use the cat, more, or less commands to quickly display the information you need. These commands are discussed in depth in Lesson 7, "Reading Files."

```
>more /usr/doc/at-3.1.7/Copyright

This package was debianized by Thomas Koenig ig25@rz.
↪uni-karlsruhe.de on
Thu, 20 Feb 1997 17:33:12 +0100.

Original version.
```

Nothing too exciting, but there's no telling what you might learn if you
poke around.

HOWTO INFORMATION

Documentation about individual programs is useful, but you might also be
interested in how to complete certain tasks on your system, such as configuring a soundcard. Linux provides a comprehensive HOWTO database
that contains information on everything, including configuring your system to use 3D accelerators or soundcards. The HOWTO files are located
in the /usr/doc directory, in a subdirectory called /usr/doc/HOWTO.

To see the available HOWTO files, list the HOWTO:

```
>ls /usr/doc/HOWTO

3Dfx-HOWTO
AX25-HOWTO
Access-HOWTO
Alpha-HOWTO
Assembly-HOWTO
Benchmarking-HOWTO
BootPrompt-HOWTO
Bootdisk-HOWTO
Busmouse-HOWTO
CD-Writing-HOWTO
...
```

Use **more**, **less**, or **cat** to display any of the files that might be of interest to you. For example, to display information on setting up a 3Dfx accelerator card, type the following:

```
>more /usr/doc/HOWTO/3Dfx-HOWTO
```

Complete configuration instructions will be displayed. There are a very large number of HOWTO files available, so you should be sure to check to see if a HOWTO help file is available for any problems you encounter.

HTML HELP INFORMATION

Much of the HOWTO information, as well as other documentation, is available in HTML format. Viewing the documentation in HTML format using the Lynx browser might be a more pleasant experience. You can use any browser you'd like to display the information. Lynx, however, is usable from the command line, and is extremely fast. The HTML version of the HOWTO documentation is located in the /usr/doc/HOWTO/other-formats/html.

For example, to view the 3Dfx-HOWTO file in HTML format, you could do this

```
>lynx /usr/doc/HOWTO/other-formats/html/3Dfx-HOWTO.html
```

The text-based Lynx browser loads and displays the HTML formatted version of the 3Dfx HOWTO document.

 Format Varieties   Documentation can come in formats other than plain text or HTML. If you stumble across a file ending in .ps, .eps, or something else that isn't easily readable, check out the section, "File Formats," in Lesson 7.

OTHER INFORMATION SOURCES

Linux is growing quickly, and so are the resources that provide support and information. Searching for Linux using any Web search engine will yield thousands of sites offering information on the subject. Here are a few Web sites and newsgroups that you might want to use as starting points for your search.

THE LINUX HOME PAGE

The Linux home page is an excellent starting point for anything related to the operating system. Links are provided to vendors, applications, events, and other Linux goodies. Check out their home page at
`http://www.linux.org/`.

THE LINUX DOCUMENTATION PROJECT

The Linux Documentation Project is a continuously updated collection of information related to Linux. The LDP contains FAQs (frequently asked questions), HOWTOs, and other documentation related to the installation and maintenance of Linux-based systems. You might have a copy of the LDP already installed on your system in the /usr/doc/LDP directory. To view the most current information, however, you should check the online LDP reference, which is located at `http://sunsite.unc.edu/LDP/`.

NEWSGROUPS

Newsgroups provide a less structured approach to finding information, but you'll be surprised with the amount of support you can get from complete strangers. Whatever your need, there is a Linux newsgroup that will provide answers. To get started, take a look at

- `comp.os.linux.answers`

- `comp.os.linux.setup`

- `comp.os.linux.misc`

THE KDE HELP SYSTEM

If you are using KDE for most of your day-to-day work, you'll be glad to know that KDE has its own built-in HTML help system that is extremely well-integrated into the KDE environment.

Tips of All Sorts   If you don't want to use the full-blown help system, KDE's *ToolTips* might help you. ToolTips are quick little blips of information that are displayed when you pass your cursor over an icon or menu selection. Not all applications support ToolTips, but if you don't know what something does, pass your cursor over it, wait a few seconds, and see if one appears.

Each application has its own Help menu that is laid out according to the KDE specification, which maintains consistency across all KDE applications.

To access the Help viewer from within an application, select **Contents** from the **Help** menu. Figure 2.1 shows the help available from within Karm, the KDE personal information manager.

FIGURE **2.1**   KDE has an integrated HTML-based help system.

The KDE Help viewer is a full-fledged HTML viewer. You can navigate through the help files by clicking the links, as you would in any Web browser.

 Tip Trick Up Your Sleeve   Because the KDE help and file browser is really just an HTML browser, you can use the KDE browser to view any of the other Linux HTML documentation. Type the URL of the file you want to view into the top of the browser window and press **Enter**.

SUMMARY

There are many help resources available for Linux. Depending on your needs, you can approach your search for information several ways. The methods you should now be familiar with are

- **Linux manual pages**—Use the `man` command to display full information about a specific command. The `apropos`, `man -k`, `man -f`, and `whatis` commands can display summary information and search for a specific type of command.

- **Built-in help**—Many programs have built-in help that can be displayed with a command-line argument, usually `--help` or `-h`.

- **/usr/doc directory**—Documentation for many programs and tasks is located in the /usr/doc directory. HTML-formatted information is also available in this directory.

- **Online resources**—The Linux home page and Documentation Project provide excellent starting points when wading through the mountains of online Linux information. The `comp.os.linux` newsgroups are also extremely useful for hard-to-find answers.

- **KDE Help system**—KDE provides excellent built-in help for most of its applications. Simply select **Contents** from the **Help** menu that is located in each application.

LESSON 3
THE GRAPHICAL USER INTERFACE

In this lesson you will learn the basics of the X Windows GUI, along with enough information to get you started on configuring and customizing your environment.

While Linux can be accessed via a command-line interface from the console, there is an easier way. On top of the command-line interface, a variety of graphical user interfaces (GUIs) are available. A few of these GUIs are proprietary, but the majority conform to an open-standard interface called the X Window System, or X Windows. Some manufacturers have extended the X Windows standard with proprietary enhancements, which can cause parts of the interface to be incompatible with remote display on other Linux and UNIX systems. However, the general principles are similar, and a familiarity with one interface translates well to the others. If you can learn X Windows under Linux, you should have no problem applying that knowledge to commercial UNIX systems.

X WINDOWS BASICS

Unlike the Macintosh and MS-Windows environments, X Windows is a system that provides a set of interface display functions. Linux provides a free distribution of X Windows called XFree86. Currently it supports the latest X Windows revision, 6.2, and just about any video card that is available for the Intel platform.

X Marks the Spot   X Windows is usually referred to as X#, where # is the major revision number, or X#Rn where # is the major revision number and *n* is the minor revision. As of this writing, X11R6 is the current version, but it is generally referred to as X11—or, just X.

X Windows provides facilities for programs to display windows, buttons, and other user-interactive widgets. The interface is actually implemented as a type of server program running on the computer. Client programs that want to make use of X Windows display functionality contact the server and make requests asking it to perform certain display functions. It does not matter to either the client or server application whether they are running on the same machine or separated by miles of network—the client makes display requests and the server tries to honor them.

An additional difference between personal-computer windowing systems and X Windows is the fact that the look and feel of the interface is controlled by a separate program, rather than by the X Windows server. In the X Windows model, the X server is responsible for handling client display requests, such as requests for displaying windows. Unless a client specifically draws a title bar for itself, X won't give it one. A separate program must be run to create title bars and to actually manage user interactions, such as moving windows around, iconizing or minimizing windows, or providing application-dock functionality.

STARTING X WINDOWS

On many Linux boxes, you, or the system administrator, might have configured X so that it starts automatically when the machine boots. If your system does not automatically start X, you will need to start it manually after you log in. The two most common ways to do this are the xinit program and startx shell script. Startx (and its variants) is usually a shell script that automates some of the calls to xinit, and would be a good place to start browsing if you're curious about how things are done and what options are available. (Shell scripts are covered in Lesson 14, "Basic Shell Scripting.")

After the X server itself starts, you will need to start some X applications. Usually, a default set of these is started by the automatic execution of the .xinitrc file located in your home directory. Some Linux distributions don't use this file. Your system administrator can always change the default configuration. If you can't locate .xinitrc, you might find that your system remembers what windows you have open and where they are positioned between logins "automagically."

The .xinitrc file (if present) contains a series of lines similar to the following:

```
#!/bin/sh
xrdb -load $HOME/.X11defaults
xscreensaver -timeout 10 &
xterm -geometry 80x30+10+10 &
```

If this in fact was your .xinitrc file, when you started X11, the .xinitrc file would:

- **Line 1**—Run itself via the bourne shell, sh.

- **Line 2**—Load the server resource database (discussed later in this lesson) from the file .X11defaults in your home directory.

- **Line 3**—Start the xscreensaver command with a 10-minute timeout, and then place it in the background.

- **Line 4**—Start an xterm (terminal), which is 80 characters wide by 30 characters high and place it 10 pixels from the top and left of your screen.

You'll see more examples of command-line options to X programs later in this lesson.

USING X WINDOWS

The look and feel of X Windows is mostly the responsibility of the particular window manager you've chosen to run. (You'll learn more about window managers and some of their options later in this lesson.) It is likely that you'll find a number of constants between the different window managers. Some of these consistent features will be familiar to anyone who has previously used a computer with a mouse: for example, pointing and clicking and dragging and dropping. A few managers, however, are likely to be new to users familiar with the Macintosh and MS-Windows environments. The significant things to remember are

- **X is designed for a three-button mouse**—Most X software makes use of the left button for pointing, clicking, and selection. The center button is used for X11 general functions such as moving or resizing windows. X uses the right button for application-specific functions such as opening in-application pop-up menus. Of course, any application is capable of modifying these uses, so examination of the documentation is always appropriate. If you only have a two-button mouse, don't worry. Linux allows you to configure a two-button mouse to emulate a third button when both buttons are clicked simultaneously.

- **X has the concept of** *focused input*—On the Macintosh or MS-Windows platforms, if you type on the keyboard, you generally expect the typing to appear in whatever window or dialog box is foremost on the screen. This isn't the case with X Windows. In X, the window manager has the option of *focusing* your input anywhere it chooses. Most window managers can be configured to focus input on the foremost window, focus input on a selected window (X does not have to be the foremost window), or focus input on whichever window the cursor is over. The last option, while least like the interface you might be familiar with, is usually considered to be the most powerful. With the window manager configured so that focus follows the cursor, you can direct typing into a mostly hidden window (for example, to start a non-interactive program) by moving the cursor over any visible part of the mostly hidden window and typing. No need to waste time to bring that window to the front, type the command, and then shuffle it back underneath whichever window it was that you really wanted to work in.

If Your Input Vanishes   If you're typing and you notice that what you're typing isn't appearing where you think it should be, chances are you have your input focused in some other window. Check to make certain that your cursor is where it belongs, or, if your system is configured for Click to Focus, ensure that you've clicked where you intend to type. It's very easy to get confused when moving between platforms using different input focus methods.

In X, the window manager or any other program can attach arbitrary commands to arbitrary user actions. For example, when a user right-clicks the title bar, a program might attach the action of displaying a menu. The window manager might pop up a variety of menus when the user left-, right-, or center-clicks in the empty background of the windowing system (or shift-left, shift-right, or shift-center clicks—the possibilities are endless). One popular terminal program, xterm, pops up its configuration menus when the user holds down the Ctrl key and left-, right-, or center-clicks in the window. Some window managers attach a standard menu with common commands such as Close and Resize to each application's title bar. Others attach these functions to pop-up menus or buttons in the title bar. Even among different releases of Linux you will find variations in program behavior; local configuration options can exert a significant influence over the interface. The best advice on how to find any particular option or command is to read the available documentation and to ask other local users.

Most window managers have the capability to *iconize* or minimize windows. Because the actual display of the client program's windows isn't handled by the client, the X server and window manager are free to make some useful contributions to the user experience. One of these contributions is that when the client requests a window with particular characteristics, the server isn't obliged to represent the window that way to the user. It is required only to treat it as though it had those characteristics. For example, this allows the server to scale the window arbitrarily, or to shrink it down and treat it as an icon. If you're familiar with the idea of a taskbar or application dock, you can think of iconized windows as windows that have been minimized, but which you can store anywhere onscreen.

CONFIGURING X WINDOWS

Most configuration of X Windows is handled by a server resource data-base. When a client makes a request of the server, the server checks this database to determine user preferences for that client. The server resource database is loaded on a per-user basis via the xrdb command, which should be executed automatically after starting X11. Xrdb loads configuration information from a dot file, usually named .Xdefaults. (Dot files are discussed in Lesson 16, "Modifying the User Environment.") .Xdefaults usually contain lines similar to the following:

```
xbiff*onceOnly:              on
xbiff*wm_option.autoRaise:   off
xbiff*mailBox:               /usr/spool/mail/mymail
```

If you included these lines in your .Xdefaults file you would be telling your X server that if xbiff (an X11 program that notifies you when you have new mail) starts, it needs to set certain options.

- **Line 1**—Sets an xbiff specific option regarding the frequency of ringing the bell to notify you.

- **Line 2**—Sets an option regarding the window manager's treatment of xbiff. It specifically tells the system not to bring xbiff to the front if it's behind other windows when it needs to notify you. (Remember, X11 provides the display and a separate program provides management of things such as window controls.)

- **Line 3**—Tells xbiff where to find the mailbox that it's supposed to look at.

Because each client supports different options and allows the window manager different levels of control, you'll need to consult each client's documentation to learn what you can configure and what you need to do to configure it.

In addition to the server resources database, clients frequently have com-mand-line options that can control the client's interaction with X11. Start an xterm with the following command:

```
> xterm -fg "black" -bg "white" -fn 6x10 -geometry 85x30+
➥525+1
```

While starting an xterm, this command also sets the foreground color to black, the background color to white (black text on a white window), and tells the system to use a 6×10 point font. It also sets the geometry information such that the window is 85 characters wide and 30 characters high, and is placed 525 pixels from the left edge of the screen and 1 pixel down from the top.

Again, different programs have different options available and your local documentation is your best source for up-to-date information on your exact configuration.

WINDOW MANAGERS

Because X Windows provides only rudimentary user interface component display functionality, an additional program is required to provide a useful user interface. This program is the window manager. Depending on the distribution of Linux you are running, you might have a number of options for different window managers. Each provides slightly different features with accordingly different strengths and weaknesses.

twm

One of the most common and least-featured window managers is twm. twm, shown managing the display in Figure 3.1, provides very basic window management functions. Fortunately, it is present or available on almost all Linux implementations. If you work in a multiplatform environment with different flavors of Linux or UNIX, you might find twm to be convenient, because your configuration can be identical on all the machines. For its simplicity, twm also provides one of the most user-extendable interfaces of all the window managers. If you like, you can create your own standard buttons that appear in your twm title bars and execute arbitrary commands. You can build your own pop-up menus, automatically execute commands when the cursor enters windows, customize window manager colors and actions by application name and application type, and perform a host of other customizations. To start the twm window manager, execute twm after starting X (you should be able to do this automatically in your .xinitrc file). The control file for all this customization is named .twmrc and should be located in your home directory.

Iconized Active Applications   twm Title Bar

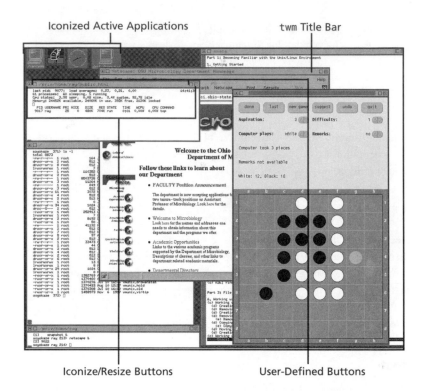

Iconize/Resize Buttons   User-Defined Buttons

FIGURE 3.1   twm managing an X Windows session.

As you can see in Figure 3.1, twm allows you to have a number of windows open at once. During window layering, even though windows might be partially covered by one another, you can focus input to the hidden windows, allowing you to work in any open window. Active applications that have been iconized can be clicked to be expanded once again to their normal size.

OTHER WINDOW MANAGERS

Other window managers you might encounter include

- mwm—The Motif window manager. Many commercial window managers are based on, or try very hard to emulate, mwm.

- 4dwm—The default window manager for SGIs running IRIX.

- **tvtwm**—An experimental extension of **twm** that includes the capability to set up virtual screens.

- **afterstep**—A popular Linux window manager that emulates the look and feel of the NeXT operating system.

- **fvwm95**—No one can really agree what the **f** stands for, but this window manager looks almost identical to Windows 95/98/NT.

There are many other window managers, and a variety will most likely be available to you for use on your machine. After you've investigated your options you can start building a custom environment that feels and behaves exactly as you want it to.

Remember, the window manager provides user interface features such as title bars. If you find yourself facing a screen that looks like Figure 3.2, it is because there is no window manager running (either it hasn't started for some reason, or it has crashed). You can try starting a window by typing **twm** if there is a terminal window open that is accepting keyboard input (directing keyboard input to a particular window is also a window manager function). If not, you'll need to exit the X Window System and modify your startup files to start the window manager of your choice immediately after starting the X server.

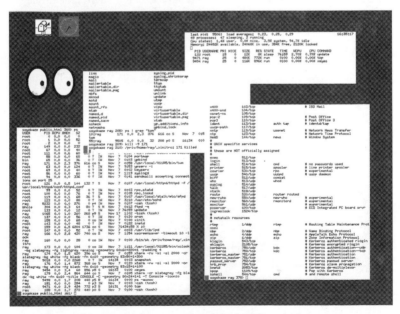

FIGURE 3.2   This X Windows session has lost its window manager.

DESKTOP ENVIRONMENTS

Historically, window managers have only been used to manage the user's screen. However, a new type of application is emerging and functions not only as a window manager in the classical sense, but also provides additional functionality to the user. These desktop environments typically provide sophisticated window management as well as a sort of desktop, which is reminiscent of the MS-Windows or Macintosh interface. The desktop frequently includes file management functionality, the capability to create and use icons to launch applications, and an integrated suite of graphical tools for the management and configuration of the computer.

As Linux vendors try to make their machines more convenient to use, you can expect these desktop environments to become more sophisticated, but even today the power and simplicity are quickly approaching that of the popular personal computer interfaces.

While some of the industry heavy-hitters like Sun and SGI have weighed in with significant offerings such as OpenWindows and the IRIX desktop, one of the most significant contributions is being made by a non-profit Internet collaborative effort that is developing the freeware product KDE. KDE is a freely available and downloadable desktop environment that is compatible with a wide range of Linux distributions.

KDE

KDE stands for the K Desktop Environment, and according to the authors the K doesn't stand for anything. KDE continues to be developed and within the past two years has matured into a very flexible and attractive environment for Linux users. Some distributions of Linux, such as Caldera's OpenLinux, include KDE.

 Compatibility According to the KDE FAQ, KDE is currently known to support Linux, Solaris, FreeBSD, IRIX and HP-UX, and is expected to be compatible on almost anything that uses the gnu gcc compiler.

KDE provides a sophisticated window manager with convenient extensions such as multiple virtual screens, user-customizable menus, and a facility to automatically remember programs and their placement on the screen between login sessions.

In addition, KDE provides a desktop environment that supports, among other things, icons for files and directories, an application dock, and a quick launch button bar. As you can see in Figure 3.3, the user interface that KDE provides is significantly more user-friendly than the twm (and other typical window manager) interfaces.

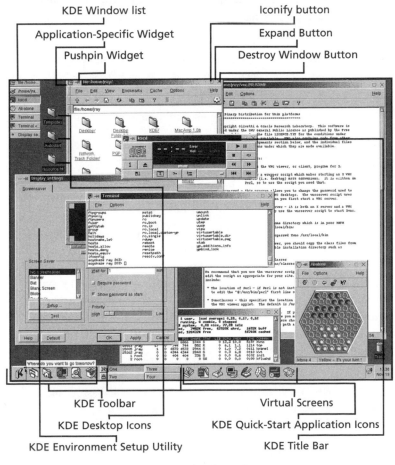

FIGURE 3.3   KDE makes X Windows friendly.

Let's take a look at some of the KDE window features:

- **KDE Window list**—Shows you a list of all windows available currently, even if they're completely hidden onscreen.

- **Application-specific widget**—The leftmost widget on the title bar. Its functions are specific to the application associated with the window.

- **Pushpin widget**—This button locks the window to your display, making it available on any virtual screen you access.

- **Iconify, expand, and destroy Window buttons**—These buttons give you control of the window—minimize it, maximize it, or close it entirely.

- **KDE quick-start application icons**—Puts you one click away from your most frequently used programs.

- **KDE toolbar**—This panel includes pop-up menus to start programs, select windows, and configure your environment.

- **KDE Environment Setup utility**—Allows you to control such things as your screen saver, display settings, and so on.

- **KDE desktop icons**—These icons "live" on your desktop and represent files, directories, or applications.

In addition to user interface sophistication, KDE provides an integrated suite of tools for configuring your machine and your user interface, and offers a set of useful point-and-click interfaces to general Linux programs and utilities. Some of these utilities will be discussed in other lessons, so if you're using a desktop environment of some sort already, pay attention to these sections to see how KDE, and desktop environments in general, can make your life easier.

If you're looking for a way to make your Linux experience feel even more like your personal computer, ask your administrator to make sure that KDE is installed on your system. The KDE Web site and associated downloads are located at http://www.kde.org.

SUMMARY

In this lesson you learned about the background of the X Window System, and how it can be customized. There are hundreds of X Windows applications that are installed with a basic Linux distribution. Understanding X Windows will enable you to take advantage of these graphics-based tools.

- **X Windows is based on a client/server model**—The client runs anywhere you want it to and makes display requests. The server runs on the machine with the display screen and attempts to honor those requests.

- **The X Windows System requires a window manager to implement user interface conveniences such as title bars.**

- **X Windows mice can behave in strange ways**—If at first you don't succeed, click and click again.

- **X Windows can focus keyboard input to a window in a number of different ways**—Pay attention to where your cursor is.

- **The advent of desktop environments is bringing application icons to the world of X Windows.**

For all the power of desktop environments, and all the automation of newer window managers, their configurations are usually stored in ugly text files in your home directory. The KDE software keeps most of its configuration in files stored under the .kde directory within your home directory. If you want to duplicate your environment from one machine to another, this is a good place to start.

LESSON 4
THE FILE
SYSTEM

In this lesson you'll learn the basics of the Linux file system and a few con-
venient tricks to make your life easier as you use Linux.

To the novice, the Linux file system can appear to be a strange and uninvit-
ing place—so many files, and you with just a command line to type at.
Bear skin and stone knife time, right? Wrong. While the access to the Linux
file system might initially appear cryptic and primitive, Linux provides
extremely sophisticated file access and control. This sophistication is born
of many simple commands with which more complicated commands can be
constructed.

FILE SYSTEM DESIGN

Before even the simple commands will make sense, you need to understand
a few things about the design of the Linux file system. This might not seem
like a very important part of the user experience, but the Linux file system
is a bit different than the personal computer file systems you might be
familiar with—and you will probably find the biggest differences to be to
your liking.

Linux file systems have a single root directory. Unlike Macintosh file
systems with their multiple drive icons on the desktop or Windows file
systems with their ABCs, the Linux file system has a single top-level
directory—the *root directory*. You should think of Linux files as being
arranged in a tree shape, with the root directory as the trunk. The root
directory can contain files and other directories, whereas the second-level
directories can contain more files and more directories, and so on.

The Powers of Root   Linux uses the word *root* to describe two different concepts. One is the root user, the person with absolute control over everything to do with the machine. The other is the root directory, one single specific directory on the machine that is considered to be the *base* of the file system.

You don't need to care what drives are where. Where do other drives appear, if not named by letter, or icons? With Linux, they appear simply as directories located anywhere in the file system. Odd? Not at all. Linux completely removes the notion of the hardware and the physical location of the files from the concern of the user. This might take a while to get used to, but once you do, you'll see that it makes no sense for a user to have to worry about where a file physically resides. If you know its name and where to find it in the file system, why bother worrying about what chunk of oxidized metal (that's what makes up a hard drive, by the way) it lives on? If you think about it, you'll see that this has other significant benefits. For example, if your system administrator discovers one day that he's run out of disk space to install new software, he can transparently rearrange disks and files. He can move everything out of some overloaded directory onto a new disk, mount the new disk so that it appears in the same place as the old directory, and you will never know the difference.

 Mounting a drive   The process of telling the file system that the drive exists and what directory it should appear at. On most Linux varieties, normal users can't mount drives, but if you're curious how it's done or happen to be on a system that allows normal users to mount some drives, you should see your system administrator to find out which drives you can mount and how to mount them.

You don't need to care what state your files live in. Another benefit of this abstraction is that your system administrator can cause files, directories, or drives that are physically located on distant machines to transparently appear as part of the file system on your machine. The only difference you might notice accessing files that are located remotely could be a slight slowdown due to the network. So what's this mean? If your system is set up properly, no matter where you are, what machine you sit in front of, whether you're at your main office or halfway around the world, all your files appear in the same place, and all your software is where you always expect it to be.

Even if you don't care where your files are, you're always somewhere. Linux bases most of its notion of the user environment on the user "being somewhere," located and working in some particular directory. With the advent of new graphical desktop environment tools, this is becoming less of a universal concept, but it is still a good idea to keep in mind when working with Linux.

Linux commands and filenames are case-sensitive. For both the Windows and Macintosh user, this might come as quite a surprise: Linux is quite literal in its interpretation of what you type. MyFile doesn't look identical to myfile on paper, and it's not identical to Linux either. Always note the case of filenames or commands that you are trying to use.

Files have three attributes. Linux has a very simple idea of file attributes—files can be readable or not readable, writeable or not writeable, and executable or not executable. Any combination of these options is possible, though some combinations are not particularly sensible. Generally, programs should be readable and executable, and data files should be readable and possibly writeable. Linux, however, takes you at your word. If you tell it that a data file is executable, it will allow you to run your Rolodex file, and if you tell it that a program is writeable it will let you edit your word-processor as if it were a plain-text document rather than a program.

Everything belongs to somebody. Every file and directory in the Linux file system carries around with it information detailing who owns it. The owner of a file can allow or disallow access to a file for other users, or other groups of users, and can control whether the file is executable, readable, or writeable.

Now that you understand a bit about what your commands are going to be talking to, you can start learning what you need to know to get around.

NAVIGATING THE FILE SYSTEM

The most basic commands for dealing with the Linux file system are the ones for moving between directories and finding out what files are in them. Before moving between them though, it's a good idea to know where you are.

WHERE ARE YOU? pwd

The pwd (present working directory) command asks your machine to tell you what directory you're currently in. Any time you're running a command line, it's somewhere in the file system—type **pwd** and it tells you where.

For example

```
> pwd
/priv/home/ray/public_html/
```

 Path Particulars /priv/home/ray/public_html/ is a *path*. The simplest explanation of a path is the shortest set of directories through which you must travel from the root directory to get to the current file or directory. Each directory in the path is separated by a /.

THE HOME DIRECTORY

To each user, one particular directory is a special directory. This directory is your home directory. From the standpoint of navigating around the file system this directory is identical to any other, but it is significant because when you log on, it is where you will initially be. You can expect that anything in or below your home directory belongs only to you. To make your life easier, Linux doesn't require you to remember the path to your home directory. Instead, it allows you to refer to your home directory as ~, and to anybody else's home directory as ~<username>.

Now that you know where you are, the next thing you might want to know is what files are with you.

LISTING FILES

Actually, Linux will let you list the files just about anywhere (with the exception of places that you don't have permission; more on permissions in Lesson 19, "Permissions"), but the easiest place to list files from is "here"—wherever that currently happens to be.

ls

The ls command lists files. Issued without arguments, ls lists the files and subdirectories in the current directory (the same one pwd would tell you about).

For example

```
> pwd
/priv/home/ray/public_html/
> ls
cgi_bin                    test.html
images                     vrml
index.html
```

This shows that your current directory path is /priv/home/ray/public_html, and that this directory contains five things. You can't tell from this listing, but cgi_bin, images, and vrml are directories, while index.html and test.html are files.

 Covering the Bases You didn't really have to issue the pwd command to make use of the ls command in that example. It's been included for the sake of clarity. If you already know where you are in the file system, there's no reason to ask the computer to repeat it for you.

If you'd like to list the files in some directory other than the current directory, for example the files in the root directory, you can issue the ls command with a directory option.

1. Determine the name of the directory you want to list.

2. Issue the ls command as **ls *<directory name>***

For example, if you wanted to list the contents of the root directory /, you would type:

```
> ls /
CDROM                   lib
bin                     priv
core                    tmp
dev                     vmlinux
etc                     usr
include                 var
```

Everything here is a directory, except vmlinux, which is the piece of software at the most basic heart of Linux, and core, which is an error file that really should be thrown away.

Filename Facts   Remember that Linux filenames, and consequently commands, are case-sensitive. Linux alphabetizes the capitals before the lowercase. This is why CDROM appears before bin.

How can you tell that they are directories? Use option ls to ask it for more information in the listing, specifically the "long" option.

Issue the command as **ls -l *<directory name>***

For example

```
total 19
lrwxr-xr-x    2 root   root      2048 Oct 21 07:46 bin -> /usr/bin
drwxr-xr-x    2 root   root      1024 Oct 15 14:28 boot
-r--r--r--    2 root   root   8503728 Oct 21 07:43 core
-rwxr-xr-x    2 root   root   1382760 Oct 21 07:43 vmlinux
drwxr-xr-x    3 root   root     21504 Dec  2 16:56 dev
drwxr-xr-x   29 root   root      4096 Dec  2 17:05 etc
drwxr-xr-x   16 root   root      1024 Nov 25 18:10 home
drwxr-xr-x    4 root   root      2048 Oct 26 16:30 lib
drwxr-xr-x    2 root   root     12288 Jul 14 13:51 lost+found
drwxr-xr-x    2 root   root      1024 May  7  1998 misc
drwxr-xr-x    4 root   root      1024 Jul 14 14:47 mnt
```

```
drwxr-xr-x   7 root   root     1024 Sep 30 13:14 opt
dr-xr-xr-x   5 root   root        0 Dec  2 11:55 proc
drwxr-xr-x  20 root   root     2048 Dec  2 16:59 root
drwxr-xr-x   3 root   root     2048 Oct 21 07:47 sbin
drwxrwxrwt   5 root   root     2048 Dec  2 17:54 tmp
drwxr-xr-x  24 root   root     1024 Oct 26 19:13 usr
lrwxr-xr-x  19 root   root     1024 Oct 26 19:37 var -> /usr/var
```

This listing might look a little convoluted at first, but the parts that are
important to understand at this point are fairly straightforward.

- First comes a line telling you how many things are in this
  directory, in this case 19.

- Next come lines detailing the contents of the directory, one
  per item.

- The 10 characters that look like random gibberish at the left of
  each line are actually the attribute information for the file. The
  first character of this tells you whether the line is for a directory—lines for which the first character is a d are for directories.
  Lines that start with a - are for normal files. Sharp observers will
  note that the lines for bin and var start with an l. This indicates
  that these are actually *links*, or alternative names for other files
  or directories (links will be discussed in greater depth later in
  this lesson). The remaining nine characters are three sets of
  three, indicating respectively the read, write, and execute status
  of the file for the file's owner, the file's group, and everybody
  else. These properties (permissions, owners, and groups) are discussed in depth in Lesson 19.

- Shortly after the 10 characters of permission information is a
  small number—don't worry to much about this number, it is the
  number of hard links to a particular file. This is unimportant to
  most everyone except the die-hard UNIX fans.

- Each line contains root. This is the owner of the file or directory. In this case, the root user owns everything in this directory.
  This is immediately followed by the name of the group that the
  file belongs to. In this example, the group is also root.

- Next comes a number, sometimes small and sometimes large.
  This is the amount of disk space that the file or directory occu-
  pies. For directories, it's not the space that the contents of the

directory occupy, but the space occupied by the data file that controls the directory. This value is in bytes. As you can see, the directories take up very little room (although their contents might be a different story), while vmlinux takes roughly 1.4MB, and that pesky core file (which should be deleted) is taking up 8.5MB.

- After the file size comes the date of the most recent modification of the file. If the file was modified in the last year, the date and time are given; otherwise, a date and year are given.

- Finally comes the filename. You will note that the filenames are identical to the names given by the version of ls from the previous example, with the exception of bin and var, which have a funny pointer that points to a path. As previously mentioned, these are actually alternative names for other directories, and the pointer is pointing at the path that they are linked to.

By now perhaps you have noticed that the total line claims that this directory contains 14 items, but that only 12 appear in the listing. This is because Linux, as a courtesy, hides some files from the user unless they are specifically asked for. Files whose names begin with a "." (dot) are not shown by default. Typically, control and configuration files which you would not want to see cluttering up your directory listing are named starting with a dot so that you don't have to see them in everyday use. Nevertheless, if you want to see them, all you have to do is ask. In this case, use the all option for ls.

For example

```
>ls -al /
total 19
drwxr-xr-x  2 root    root          8 Oct 15 14:28 .
-rwx------  2 root    root         42 Oct 21 07:43 .login
lrwxr-xr-x  2 root    root       2048 Oct 21 07:46 bin -> /usr/bin
drwxr-xr-x  2 root    root       1024 Oct 15 14:28 boot
-r--r--r--  2 root    root    8503728 Oct 21 07:43 core
-rwxr-xr-x  2 root    root    1382760 Oct 21 07:43 vmlinux
drwxr-xr-x  3 root    root      21504 Dec  2 16:56 dev
drwxr-xr-x 29 root    root       4096 Dec  2 17:05 etc
drwxr-xr-x 16 root    root       1024 Nov 25 18:10 home
drwxr-xr-x  4 root    root       2048 Oct 26 16:30 lib
drwxr-xr-x  2 root    root      12288 Jul 14 13:51 lost+found
```

```
drwxr-xr-x   2 root    root          1024 May  7  1998 misc
drwxr-xr-x   4 root    root          1024 Jul 14 14:47 mnt
drwxr-xr-x   7 root    root          1024 Sep 30 13:14 opt
dr-xr-xr-x   5 root    root             0 Dec  2 11:55 proc
drwxr-xr-x  20 root    root          2048 Dec  2 16:59 root
drwxr-xr-x   3 root    root          2048 Oct 21 07:47 sbin
drwxrwxrwt   5 root    root          2048 Dec  2 17:54 tmp
drwxr-xr-x  24 root    root          1024 Oct 26 19:13 usr
lrwxr-xr-x  19 root    root     1024 Oct 26 19:37 var -> /usr/var
```

You will note that two new lines have appeared in the listing: a line for a file named cryptically ".", and a line for a file named .login. The .login file is a typical Linux configuration file, and you should expect to see files of this nature in any directory used as a home directory. The "." file might be a little less expected; however, it is quite normal. The directory "." exists in every directory on a Linux machine and is essentially synonymous with the current directory. For example, the command ls, and the command ls . will produce identical results, because ls defaults to listing the current directory, and "." is the current directory.

The root directory / is unique in that it does not have a directory named ".." in it. The directory ".." is synonymous with "the directory one above this one." Therefore, if you're currently in /home/ray/public_html, ls .. will produce a listing of /home/ray.

The ls command has many options in addition to the ones discussed here: options for sorting, tabulating the data, and adding flags to the "short" listing to show the file's attributes. Beyond the -l and -a options discussed earlier, the next most useful are the -F option, which indicates file attributes, and the -R option, which recursively lists all files below the specified directory.

CHANGING DIRECTORIES: cd

Now that you know how to find out where you are, and what's around you, it's time to wander around a bit. To move from one directory to another use the Linux command cd. If you want to move from wherever you currently are to another directory

1. Determine where you currently are (use the pwd command if you don't already know).

2. Pick a directory you would like to go to (/usr/local for this example).

3. Issue the cd command as **cd <directory name>**

For example

```
> pwd
/home/ray/public_html
> cd /usr/local
> pwd
/usr/local
```

The final pwd shows /usr/local as the current directory, which is exactly what you wanted.

pushd AND popd

An even more powerful way of changing between directories is to make use of the directory *stack*.

 Stack In computer-speak, a stack is a type of data storage that works for data much like a stack of dishes. With the dish stack, dishes can only be added to the pile or taken off the pile from the top, and the most recently added plate is the first to be removed. Data storage stacks work in exactly the same way. Data is pushed onto the stack, burying previous data, and popped off of the stack uncovering previous data.

If you are currently in one directory and would like to change temporarily to another, there is an easier way to do it than with two cd commands. By making use of the pushd command, you can place the current directory on the directory stack and change your current directory to the new directory. When you are ready to return to your previous directory, use popd to get your old directory back.

If you would like to change from your current directory to another, and return automatically, make use of the pushd and popd commands as follows.

1. Decide where you want to go.

2. Issue the pushd command as **pushd <directoryname>**

3. You will now be in your new directory and can work here for as long as you like. Your previous directory is waiting for you on the stack.

4. When you are finished and want to return to your previous directory, issue the popd command as **popd**.

For example

```
> pwd
/usr/local
> pushd /var/log
/var/log /usr/local
> pwd
/var/log
```

...now you can work here as long as you like.

```
> popd
/usr/local
> pwd
/usr/local
```

You now know almost everything about navigating around the Linux file system, but before going on to other topics there's one additional variation that you should be aware of.

ABSOLUTE AND RELATIVE PATHS

Up to this point, all paths you have been working with have been *absolute* paths—that is, paths starting with the root directory and ending in a file or directory name. In real life you would quickly find this annoying, and so Linux provides the concept of a relative path as well. Relative paths are "relative" to the current directory. With the addition of relative paths to your toolkit, if the current directory is /usr/local/ and you want to be in the directory /usr/local/bin/, you have the option of issuing two different cd commands. You can type either **cd /usr/local/bin** or **cd bin**; either will result in your new current directory being /usr/local/bin. You can also use the directory element .. discussed earlier as a relative path component. If, for example, you are in /usr/local/bin, and want to be in /usr/local/lib, you have a choice of cd **/usr/local/lib**, or cd **../lib**.

Path Do's and Don'ts   All absolute paths must start with "/"; no relative paths do.

By this point, you know how to find out where you are, what files are in what directories, and how to move around to different directories. Now it's time to learn a few tricks.

FILENAME EXPANSION IN SUPPORTED SHELLS

Some shells (tcsh and bash being the most prevalent) support *filename expansion*. Essentially this is a way of getting the shell to do some of your typing for you. If your shell supports filename expansion, to use this feature you need to press the **Tab** key after typing the beginning (hopefully enough of the beginning to uniquely identify the file) of the filename or directory name. For example, if you want to edit a preexisting file named mybigfile.dat, which is located in your current directory, you might issue the command: **emacs mybi Tab**. (*Emacs* is an editor that is discussed in Lesson 8, "Text Editing.") If you have no other files that start with the characters mybi in the current directory, the shell will automatically complete the filename for you. If you do have other files that start with mybi, the shell will beep at you, and you'll have to type some more of the filename to make it unique before trying the **Tab** key again.

Remember, all these techniques can be used together. If you're working in /usr/local/bin and suddenly remember that you forgot to edit some files in /usr/local/myincludes, you could get there with **pushd ../myin Tab**, and back again with **popd**.

NAVIGATING THE FILE SYSTEM USING KDE

If you find moving around the command line awkward, you'll be happy to know that KDE provides a very user-friendly way to navigate the file system. Similar to Windows 98, KDE's file management system is also based on the philosophy that "everything is a Web page." Each file manager window supports the full functionality of a normal Windows or

Mac OS window, but is also a full-fledged Web browser. Breaking slightly from the double-click model that you're undoubtedly used to, KDE only requires a single-click to perform its actions.

SIMPLE KDE ACTIONS

In KDE, files are represented with icons that usually indicate the file type. Directories are shown as folders. Double-clicking a directory is similar to using the cd command to get to that directory from the command line; a new window should open up to display the contents of that directory. Figure 4.1 shows a KDE file manager window.

 Navigating Your Files   Notice that the file manager window displays the URL of the directory it is showing. Because each window is a Web browser, you can substitute a Web or FTP address into the URL field, and KDE will immediately take you there—assuming you have an Internet connection, of course!

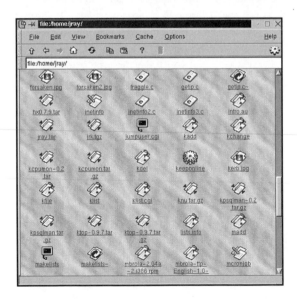

FIGURE 4.1   KDE looks and acts similar to other popular desktop environments.

To move or copy files between locations, you can drag files from location to location as you'd expect. A pop-up menu appears at the end of the drag asking if you'd like to copy or move the files; this is an example of a *contextual menu*, which appears when an action is performed within a certain context.

To delete files, drag the files you want to erase to the **Trash** icon. Click the icon with your right mouse button and choose **Empty Trash Bin** to complete the action.

New folders can be created by right-clicking in the location where you want the folder to appear, and then choosing **New** from the pop-up contextual menu and **Folder** from its submenu.

 Getting Home If you need to get to your home directory in KDE, look for the icon of a folder with a little house on top of it. Clicking this icon opens a KDE file manager window showing your home directory.

If you spend a few minutes playing around with KDE, you'll find that its simplicity and elegance are on par with commercial desktop operating systems. If you've previously worked with personal computers, you might find it a bit difficult to believe, but in the world of Linux, most of the truly great software is user-written, community supported, based on open standards, and completely free, which scares the jeebees out of the big OS manufacturers.

There's quite a bit to explore, so, if you're running a KDE system, take a few minutes to look around before you continue on to Lesson 5, "Finding Files."

SUMMARY

Navigating the Linux file system is one of the primary skills you should practice. This lesson has given you the basic skills to work within the file system and the KDE environment. If you have any problems with this material, please practice it before moving to the next lesson. Let's review some of this lesson's specifics:

- **Linux abstracts the physical location of the data**—Don't worry about where your data and software physically reside—if your system administrator is doing his or her job, it doesn't matter.

- **Linux is case-sensitive**—Pay careful attention to case, especially if you're transferring files between a Linux machine and a personal computer.

- **Linux files have attributes of readability, writeability, and executeability**—You can set the attributes of a file that you own so that you cannot execute it, write it, and read it, but you do not want to do this.

- **The pwd command tells you where you are.**

- **The ls command tells you what files are in a directory.**

- **The cd command take you places.**

- **The pushd command remembers where you were, and the popd command takes you back again.**

- **Use relative paths when you can**—If the directory is near your current directory, it's usually much more convenient to use a relative path from your current directory than to use the absolute path from /.

- **Remember that all these features and commands work together**—Linux is about combining many small programs and features that do small parts of the job you need done into a convenient tool that performs precisely as you want it to.

- **Desktop environments can make your life easier**—They automate some of the routine day-to-day tasks and provide a friendly face for some of the more difficult ones. If your system doesn't have KDE, don't fret; chances are that either KDE can be installed on it (if you're nice enough to your system administrator), or it already comes with a nice desktop environment with comparable capabilities.

LESSON 5
FINDING FILES

In this lesson you will learn to use some of the built-in Linux search tools to locate files.

In Lesson 4, "The File System," you learned how to list the files in directories and navigate from directory to directory. You probably also notice that there are a lot of files included in a standard Linux distribution. You're certain to run into the situation where you know the name of a file you want to use, but have no idea where its located. Rather than using the cd and ls commands to navigate your way through the entire file system, you can use some of Linux's search utilities to help locate what you need.

FINDING FILES

In order to locate a file, you need to know something about it: a portion of its name, when it was created, or perhaps its size. Armed with these pieces of information, you can dispatch the find command and let it scour the file system looking for matches to your query.

FINDING A FILE BY NAME

The most common type of search is by file name. You've probably used a find file command on other operating systems that works similarly. You supply the filename or portion of the filename to be found, and the system returns a list of matches. To search for a file by name, do the following:

1. Determine the name of the file you want to search for. If you want, you can include wildcards in the search for the filename.

2. Choose a starting directory for the search. If you want to search the entire file system, the starting directory should be /.

3. Invoke the find command as: **find <starting directory> -name <filename>**

4. Depending on the speed and size of the file system you're searching, be prepared to wait a while!

Search Errors   If you're searching the entire file system, you're likely to encounter errors such as:

```
find: /home/ftp/bin: Permission denied
find: /home/ftp/etc: Permission denied
```

This is entirely normal, and shouldn't be cause for alarm. The system is telling you that you're trying to search files that are not yours. If you confine the search to your directory, which can be represented to the system as ~/, you will not see any of these errors.

For example

```
>find / -name sound
/usr/src/linux-2.0.34/drivers/sound
/usr/src/linux-2.0.35/drivers/sound
/var/lock/subsys/sound
/etc/rc.d/init.d/sound
```

The system has responded to my request by finding four different files named sound. Because I chose to search the entire file system, the search took over a minute; there are hundreds of directories and thousands of filenames that were just processed.

FINDING A FILE BY DATE

Imagine you just created a document file on the system but you can't remember its name. How in the world can you find it? One possible solution is to search by time, finding files that are younger than a certain time. To search for a file by its creation date

1. Determine the relative age of your file in days.

2. Choose a starting directory for the search. Remember, / searches the entire file system, while ~/ searches just your personal directory.

3. Invoke find using the -ctime option: **find**
   <starting directory> -ctime <days old>

For example

```
>find ~/ -ctime 2
/home/jray/getip.c
/home/jray/a.out
/home/jray/getip2.c
/home/jray/.saves-8395-postoffice
```

Here, I've searched my home directory for files that have been modified in the last two days (48 hours). Hopefully one of these four files is the one that I was trying to find.

FIND A FILE BY SIZE

The advantage of finding a file by size might not be immediately obvious until your system begins to run out of room. Linux and other UNIX-based operating systems often save a file called core when a program crashes. This is referred to as a core dump. The core file contains all the information in memory when the program crashed and can be used by the programmers to debug what went wrong. Usually they can be erased unless you'd like to try debugging the program yourself. The problem with these files is that they tend to get written in directories that you might not be aware of, and silently consume drive space without you even knowing. Of course, you can search for large files that might have been created by some other process, but finding core files is one of the primary uses for this variation of find. To search by size

1. Choose a target file size to search for. Find returns files that are greater than or equal to the size you choose.

2. Choose a starting directory.

3. Start the Find program using the -size option: **find**
   <starting directory> -size<k>

For example

```
>find ~/ -size 1024k
/home/jray/bochs/bochs-980513/core
/home/jray/postgres51/core
```

The find command you see here has located two core files in my home directory that are 1024K or more in size. If there were other large files, they would have been listed as well, but in this case, only core files were found.

There are many other command-line switches that can by used with find besides -name, -ctime, and -size. Be sure to check out the find man pages if you're interested in learning more.

QUICKLY LOCATING A FILE OR DIRECTORY BY NAME

Find is a useful utility for finding files based on a wide range of criteria. It can, however, be a bit slow when you're searching the entire file system for a particular filename. In order to speed the process up, take a look at three simple utilities that can quickly list matching filenames on your system.

locate

The locate command is very simple. Just choose the name of the file you want to search for, and supply it on the command line as an argument to locate.

For example

```
>locate sound
/etc/sysconfig/soundcard
/home/httpd/icons/sound1.gif
/home/httpd/icons/sound2.gif
/home/jray/mysql/mysql-3.21.33/mysys/mf_soundex.c
/home/jray/mysql/mysql-3.21.33/mysys/mf_soundex.o
/home/jray/postgresql/pgsql/contrib/soundex
/home/jray/postgresql/pgsql/contrib/soundex/Makefile
...
```

You'll notice that the locate command runs almost instantly and returns several hundred filenames and directories containing the word sound. The difference in speed is because it does not directly search the file system. Instead it searches a database that is built by the updatedb command. The only drawback to this approach is that the database containing the filenames is not necessarily always up-to-date. You should speak to your system administrator to find out when he or she has configured `updatedb` to run.

whereis

The `whereis` command performs a quick search on a preset number of directories and returns paths to source code, binaries, and man pages for the file you specify. It is less useful as a general Find utility than `find` or `locate`, but might still come in handy.

For example

```
>whereis time
time: /usr/bin/time /usr/include/time.h /usr/man/man2/time.2
➥/usr/man/mann/time.n
```

The `whereis` command shows that the `time` binary is located in /usr/bin/time, whereas the header file is in /usr/include/time.h. Two man page paths are also returned. If you're interested in finding where programs and their associated files are located on your machine, `whereis` might do the trick.

which

Lastly, the `which` command can also help you locate files that are contained within one of the directories specified in your PATH environment variable. Lesson 16, "Modifying the User Environment," discusses how you can go about configuring this variable. You can invoke `which` much like you did `whereis`; just supply a filename for it to find.

For example

```
>which time
/usr/bin/time
```

Linux returns the full path to the `time` command. `which` is the least configurable of the commands you've seen so far, but it is also the fastest. If you're ever trying to remember where a program is located, give `which` a shot.

FINDING FILES THAT CONTAIN A WORD OR PATTERN

One of the most powerful built-in programs in Linux is grep. The grep command enables you to quickly search through the body of files for a particular word or pattern. It comes in three flavors: grep, egrep, and fgrep. The differences between these versions are based on the complexity of the regular expressions that they can handle. (Regular expressions define a pattern of text that can be used to search files when a specific word or phrase to search for might not be known. You will learn more about regular expressions in Lesson 13, "Regular Expressions.") The fgrep command is the fastest of the three, but handles the least complex expressions. To be safe, you can always use plain grep, which should work the same in every case, on every system. So, how do you use this wonderful tool? Give it the word or pattern to look for and the files it should search:

1. Choose the word or phrase you want to locate.

2. Find the filename you want to search. If it is in another directory, you must specify the entire pathname. You can also use wildcards to search multiple files, if you want.

3. Type **grep** *<pattern to find>* *<file or files to search>* at the command prompt.

For example

```
>grep "jray" *.txt
8979-10.txt:<manager>=jray
log.txt: Access by jray on 11/12/98
kiwi.txt: jray loves to eat kiwis.  But don't you think that
➥it would be
```

This example searches for jray in any file that ends in .txt. It has turned up three files (8979-10.txt, log.txt, and kiwi.txt) that contain the string; each filename is followed by the text that contains jray. Two options you might want to consider adding to grep are -i to ignore case, and -n to display the line numbers of the match in each file. You might add these flags to the command line, immediately following the grep command.

grep is an extremely valuable tool that will become even more valuable when you later learn about regular expressions. Remember to come back to this lesson to test some of the things you'll learn in Lesson 13.

USING THE KDE FIND FEATURE

For those of you who are running KDE, you'll be glad to know that it has a built-in Find utility that offers many of the same features of the command-line versions of find and grep. KDE has provided a friendly face to these functions that should seem quite familiar to anyone who has run a search under Mac OS or Windows computers. The KDE Find utility is shown in Figure 5.1.

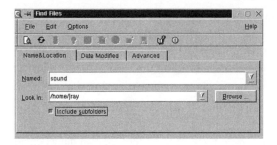

Figure 5.1   KDE provides a friendly interface to the UNIX Find and Grep utilities.

To search in KDE

1. Click the **K** toolbar icon to bring up the main KDE menu.

2. Choose **Find Files**.

3. Select the appropriate search criteria from one of the three tabs.

4. Click the small **Magnifying Glass** icon in the Find utility toolbar to locate the matching files.

There are three different tabs in the Find File utility that conduct three different types of searches:

- **Name & Location**—If you're searching for a filename, this is the tab you need to use. You can type in a partial filename and supply a starting directory for the search. This is equivalent to the find -name command you used earlier.

- **Date Modified**—Like the find -ctime option you've learned about, the Date Modified tab enables you to search your file system based on file modification dates.

- **Advanced**—The advanced options let you locate files of a specific type or search the contents of files for a word or phrase.

Of course you can continue to use the command-line utilities from within KDE, but if you're more comfortable with pointing and clicking, it's nice to know you have that option.

SUMMARY

Finding something on a Linux-based computer can be a bit difficult with the huge number of files and directories that are available to be searched. In this lesson, you learned several techniques for locating files based on their names and attributes. You learned how to search the contents of files for a particular word or phrase.

- **find**—The find command can search the entire Linux file system for a particular file based on a variety of criteria. You learned how to use it to find files based on name, creation date, and size.

- **locate**—Although useful, find isn't always an efficient way to get to your files. The locate command searches a database of filenames and instantly returns everything that matches your search request.

- **whereis**—If you're looking for a program file, its source, or its man pages, the whereis command might work for you. whereis searches a preset list of common file locations and quickly returns paths to anything it finds.

- **which**—The which function is dependant on your PATH environment variable. It searches the paths that you have specified for a particular filename.

- **grep(grep/egrep/fgrep)**—The grep command set is an extremely powerful method of searching the actual content of files for a particular word or pattern. The power of the grep command when coupled with regular expressions is incredible.

- **KDE Find utility**—KDE provides an easy-to-use interface that encompasses many of the features of find and grep.

LESSON 6

WORKING WITH FILES IN THE SHELL

In this lesson, you will learn how to perform basic file maintenance functions such as creating and deleting files and directories.

You will be unlikely to make use of any Linux commands more frequently than the file maintenance command set. Thankfully, the commands you'll use the most are very short and have only a few important options. While these commands and options might initially seem simplistic, between what you can do with them and what you'll learn about automating them in Lesson 14, "Basic Shell Scripting," you'll find that these commands can perform almost any file maintenance task you can imagine.

WORKING WITH FILES AND FOLDERS: THE COMMAND LINE

The command line is your primary interface to the Linux file system and your primary tool for creating, deleting, and rearranging your files. It's not unusual for pieces of software to provide some file creation and deletion tools, but these are rarely as powerful as the command line. Even if you intend to avoid the command line for your day-to-day work, you'll want to know about these tools.

Tweedle Dee...   When working with the command line, remember this: Filenames that you give as arguments to commands can be either relative or absolute paths. This means that if you have a command named `tweedle`, which twiddles a file, and if you type

`tweedle myfile`, or `tweedle ./myfile`, you will twiddle the file myfile in the current directory.

`tweedle ../myfile`, you will twiddle the file myfile in the directory directly above this one.

`tweedle /home/henry/myfile`, you will twiddle the file myfile in the /home/henry directory (presuming you have permission to twiddle files in that directory, of course).

Keep in mind that `tweedle` in the preceding examples is a hypothetical command with hypothetical results—UNIX has no such command. I've simply used it here to help explain a "modifies in some unspecified way" command. You can substitute any operation you'd like for `twiddle`/`tweedle`.

CREATING A NEW EMPTY FILE: touch

The `touch` command is used to update the last modified time of a file and set it to the current time. This might seem like an odd thing to want to do, but it's a very useful utility if you have an application that performs some function on files newer than a particular time.

Taking Advantage of `touch`   One place you might want to remember that you can use the `touch` command is with backup and archiving software. Many whole-system backup programs default to only backing up files that were modified since the last backup (this is called and *incremental* backup). If you want to make sure that a file is backed up, even though you've not modified it recently, you can *touch* the file to change the modification date and make it appear to have been modified at the time you touched it.

A useful side effect of touching a file is that if the file that you try to *touch* doesn't exist, touching it will cause it to be created as a new empty file.

If you need to update the modification date of a file, or create a new empty file, do the following:

1. Determine the filename or filenames of the file or files you want to either update or create.

2. Issue the touch command as **touch** *<filename> <filename>* ....

For example

> `touch myfile`

If myfile previously existed, its last modified date would now be set to the current time. If myfile did not previously exist, it would now exist as an empty file with a last modification date of the current time.

Of course, if you want to create multiple files or update the modification dates on multiple files, you could type something such as

> `touch myfile1 myfile2 myotherfile`

The result being that myfile, myfile2, and myotherfile would all have updated modification dates or be created as necessary.

 Additional Use of touch   After you become comfortable enough with Linux to start automating your work using shell scripting (discussed in Lesson 14, "Basic Shell Scripting"), you will find the touch command useful for creating *flag files* that let your scripts talk to each other. Keep the touch command in mind when thinking about uses for conditional statements.

REMOVING FILES: rm

Now that you know how to create a file, it's appropriate to learn how to get rid of it. The rm command deletes files.

The Power of rm   The rm command is a very powerful command, and one that you should be just a bit afraid of. There is not a long-time Linux user alive who has not mistyped arguments to the rm command, and then watched in considerable dismay as a large fraction of his or her file system evaporates. The rm command can remove as precisely as a scalpel or as indiscriminately as a ton of dynamite. Be careful out there!

To use the rm command to delete files, you should

1. Determine the file, or files, you want to delete.

2. Issue the rm command as: `rm <file1> <file2> <file3> ....`

You may simultaneously remove as many files as you want to. For example, if you want to delete the files myfile and myotherfile, you would use the following **rm** command:

```
> rm myfile myotherfile
```

After issuing the rm command for the files you want to delete, you might be presented with a response such as

```
remove myfile (y/n)?
```

This is rm's interactive mode, a protective measure of rm, designed to make certain that you really mean to delete the files that you specified (if you really want to, press y). Usually your system administrator will have configured your system so that rm operates in interactive mode by default. In Lesson 16, "Modifying the User Environment," you will learn how to change this default, but you would be well-advised to leave it in interactive mode until you've decided that you're comfortable with Linux.

OPTIONS TO rm
The rm command supports several useful options:

- **i**, Interactive mode—Makes rm ask you to confirm the deletion of each file before it actually deletes it. As annoying as this seems, if your system administrator hasn't configured your account to use rm in Interactive mode by default, you should get used to issuing the rm command as: rm -i <file1> <file2>...

- f, Force mode—Requests that rm carry out deletions regardless of the file permissions. Remember, you can create files and set the permissions such that even you, as the owner, can't read or write the file. If you don't use force mode, rm will ask you if you want to override the permissions whenever it tries to delete files that you can't write.

- r, Recursive mode—A very powerful option to rm, the Recursive mode is not for the faint of heart. When you issue the rm command as: rm -f <direotoryname>, rm will recursively delete the directory and all its contents. If the directory contains other directories, they will be deleted in the same manner.

CREATING A DIRECTORY: mkdir

Directories are useful for organizing files into sensible groupings. If you need to create a directory you should

1. Decide what you want to call the directory.

2. Issue the mkdir command as: mkdir <directoryname>

For example

```
> mkdir fresh_new_direcotry
```

This creates a new directory named fresh_new_direcotry, which will be located in the current directory. Unfortunately, directory was misspelled, so you'll need the next command as well. As with touch, you might want to use mkdir to create a few extra directories so you can remove them with the next command, rmdir.

REMOVING A DIRECTORY: rmdir

Old directories laying around that you no longer need aren't very helpful for organization, so occasionally you might need to delete one. The rmdir command deletes empty directories. To use it to delete a directory, you should

1. Decide which directory or directories you want out of your way.

2. Issue the rmdir command as **rmdir** *<directory1>*
   <directory2> *<directory3>*....

For example

> **rmdir fresh_new_direcotry an_old_directory/fuzzykiwi**

This deletes the misspelled directory from the preceding example, as well as the directory named fuzzykiwidir that is located in the directory named an_old_directory.

The rmdir command will not affect directories that aren't empty, so it's a convenient command to use to clean house if you've got a bunch of directories laying around. You can get it to try to delete everything in the current directory by issuing the following command:

> **rmdir ***

You're not expected to understand this syntax yet—you'll get to that in Lesson 13, "Regular Expressions." You're also likely to get dozens of error messages in response to typing this command, but the end result of issuing rmdir in this fashion is that any empty directories in this directory will go away, and nothing else will be affected.

REMOVING FILES AND DIRECTORIES AT THE SAME TIME: rm -r

Because the rmdir command only works on empty directories, you'll eventually want a way to delete a directory as well as all its contents. For this, the rm command in Recursive mode is actually the solution. If you need to delete a directory and all its contents, you should:

1. Determine the name of the directory you want to delete.

2. Issue the rm command as **rm -r** *<directoryname>*

For example, you type

> **rm -r /priv/home/henry/junkdirectory**

This removes the directory /priv/home/henry/junkdirectory, and recursively removes all its contents.

If you manage to delete your current directory (not a fun thing to do), you'll eventually end up getting error messages saying `Cannot stat current directory`, `can't stat .` and `. not found`. How long it takes UNIX to figure out that you're suddenly located "nowhere" depends on which commands you run, but you can always rescue the situation by typing: `cd ~/` to get back to your home directory.

COPYING FILES: cp

If you need to make copies of files, you will need the `cp` command. This command can either copy a single file to a new destination file or copy one or more files to a single destination directory.

To use the `cp` command to make a copy of a single file, you need to

1. Determine the source filename and the destination filename you'd like to copy it to.

2. Issue the `cp` command as **cp *<sourcefile>* *<destinationfile>***

To use the `cp` command to copy one or more files to a destination directory, you need to

1. Determine all the source filenames and the name of the destination directory. The `cp` command doesn't create the destination directory for you, so if it doesn't exist, you'll need to use the `mkdir` command first.

2. Issue the `cp` command as **cp *<source1>* *<source2>* ... *<destinationdir>***

For example

```
>cp myfile1 /priv/home/henry/myfile2
```

This copies the file myfile1 from the current directory and places a copy in /priv/home/henry/myfile2.

In its second form

```
>cp /etc/sendmail.cf /priv/home/henry/myfile2 myfile1 /tmp
```

The example shown here copies the file sendmail.cf from the directory /etc, the file myfile2 from the directory /priv/home/henry, and myfile1 from the current directory, and then places the copies in the directory /tmp.

Remember that you don't have to copy multiple files to use the "into a directory" version—just give it the one filename and the destination directory.

COPYING DIRECTORIES: cp -r

Just like the rm command has a Recursive mode for removing directories, the cp command has a Recursive mode for copying directories. If you issue the cp command with the -r option, it attempts to treat each of the source filenames as directories, and recursively copy them to the destination directory. To use the cp command in this way, you need to:

1. Determine the names of the directories you'd like to copy.

2. Issue the cp command as cp -r <source1> <source2> ... <destdir>.

For example, if you were to issue the command

```
> cp -r /var/log/httpd/logs /tmp
```

The cp command would create a new directory named logs in the directory /tmp, and makes a copy of the contents of the directory /usr/local/httpd/logs in this new /tmp/logs directory.

MOVING FILES AND DIRECTORIES: mv

If you simply need to move (rename) files, rather than copying them, you will want to use the mv command. This command uses the same two forms that the cp command does: The first moves (renames) a file from one name to another name, the second moves one or more files to a destination directory.

To use the mv command to rename a single file, you should

1. Determine the current name of the file and the name you'd prefer it to have.

2. Issue the mv command as mv <currentname> <newname>

For example, if you have a file named todays_mail, and you would like to store it away with your backed up email, you might type

```
> mv todays_mail ~/mymaildir/June10.mail
```

This command moves the file todays_mail in the current directory to the file June10.mail located in the directory ~/mymaildir. (Remember, that's the directory mymaildir located in your home directory.)

To use the mv command to move one or more files to a new location, you should

1. Determine the names of all the files you want to move and the name of the directory you'd like to move them to.

2. Issue the mv command as *mv* *<file1>* *<file2>*
   ... *<destinationdir>*

For example

```
> mv /usr/log/httpd/error_log /home/henry/myfile2 /tmp
```

This command moves the file error_log from the directory /var/log/httpd and the file myfile2 from the directory /home/henry into the directory /tmp.

Limitations to mv The mv command can also be used to move and rename directories with exactly the same syntax as using it to move and rename files—just give it directory names instead of filenames.

Unfortunately, for this task, it is a little more limited than you might like it to be. It cannot move directories between physical devices, so every now and then if you try to move a directory from one location to another, Linux's abstraction of physical devices in the file system will sneak up to bite you, and you will get an error message such as this:

```
Can't move directories across partitions
```

If this happens, your easiest solution is to use the copy command, copy the offending directory, and then delete the original.

CREATING LINKS: ln

The final file management utility you will learn about in this lesson is the command used for creating links or aliases to files. The ln command is used to create links to files so that one file can appear to be in multiple locations, and have multiple names.

To see the utility of this command, consider the situation where you want to let your friends look at your daily schedule. Daily, or weekly as appropriate, you could create a new file with your schedule and name it with the current date. Because you wouldn't want to have to constantly give your friends new filenames to check your schedule, you could just create a link named myschedule, which you would then point to whatever file contained your current schedule. Your friends could always look at myschedule to get your schedule, and you could keep your daily planner archives neatly arranged.

To use the ln command to create a link, you should

1. Determine the name of the file to which you want a link. The ln command is willing to create links to nonexistent files, which isn't particularly useful, so make certain you know the correct name of the file you want to link.

2. Determine the alternative name by which you would like be able to access the file.

3. Issue the ln command as **ln -s <*realfilename*>** **<*alternativename*>**. The -s option tells the system that this is a symbolic link. If you're interested in learning about the difference between symbolic and hard links, check out the ln man page.

For example, if you wanted to be able to easily browse your Web server log file, you might issue the command

```
> ln -s /var/log/httpd/access_log ~/weblog
```

If you were to do this, you would create a link named weblog in your home directory. This link would be an alternative name for the file /var/log/httpd/access_log.

You could work with this link almost exactly as though it were the real file. If you try to read its contents, you will read the contents of the real file. If you try to modify or edit it, you will edit the contents of the real file. If you delete the link however, you will only delete the link; the real file will remain. If you `ls -l` the link, it will show up as a filename that points to another path so that you can tell the link apart from the real file.

```
> ls -l ~/weblog
```

```
lrwxrwxr-x  1 ray       7 Nov 28   1998  weblog ->
➥/var/log/httpd/access_log
```

 Web Server Tip   One very useful place to use the `ln` command is when working with Web servers—if you're not going to be using a Web server, ignore this tip. Many Web servers serve a file named index.html by default if the user doesn't specify a filename in their URL. If you want a page to display by default, and you don't want to have to name it index.html, you can make a link to the real file named index.html, and the server will never know the difference.

SUMMARY

In this lesson, you learned a set of commands with which you can manage and arrange your files in whatever fashion you desire.

It is very important to remember that when you give a filename as an argument to a Linux command, the filename can be either a relative or absolute path to the file. If you give just the name of the file, you will be specifying a file in the current directory. If you give a partial path to the file (as in `../<filename>`, or `<directoryname>/<filename>`) you will be specifying a relative path. Finally, you can always give the absolute path from the / directory to the file. Here's a quick review of this lesson:

- **touch**—This command sets the modification date of the file to the current time. This has the effect of creating new empty files if you need them for something.

- **rm**—The `rm` command removes files. Use the `rm -i` option until you are quite certain that you know what you are doing, and then keep using it for a while longer. Recursive `rm` running in Noninteractive mode can wipe out your entire disk.

- **cp**—Copies one or more files. While a slight oversimplification, it's easiest to remember that if you start with a single file, your destination should be a single file; and if you start with multiple files, your destination must be something that can hold multiple files (such as a directory). You can also copy a single file to a directory if you like.

- **mv**—This command works a lot like cp, only it renames or moves files. The mv command cannot move directories across physical hardware boundaries, so every now and then Linux's hardware abstraction fails with this command. If this happens, look to the cp command for help.

- **ln**—The ln command creates alternative names by which a file or directory can be accessed. It's convenient for times when you need one thing to appear to be in multiple different places, or when you need to make information that you need to come from different files at different times all appear as the same filename.

Lesson 7

Reading Files

This lesson introduces you to basic commands that you can use to read files located on your computer.

Your Linux computer can be used for hundreds of applications, but no matter what the use, you're going to need to know how to do one very simple task: read files. Most Linux applications use text-based configuration files, come with text-based instruction files, and store text-based log files. Undoubtedly, you're going to want to tap into this information. Other than loading up a text editor or word processor, how can you do this? This lesson answers that question by showing you several quick commands that let you see what's inside all those files on your computer.

Viewing Files All at Once: Concatenate

The simplest way to look at files is use cat, the concatenate command. It is called concatenate because it adds to the output stream whatever is in the files it is given. You'll learn more about the output stream in Lesson 12, "Input and Output." For now, understand that this is what will be displayed onscreen. cat allows you to quickly read your files. It displays the contents of all the filenames that it is given, one immediately after another. You can use cat along with a redirection operator (you'll learn about those in Lesson 12) to create one file that holds the contents of several other files. For now, you'll use cat to display a file.

To display a file, supply cat with the file, or files you want to show as arguments to the command.

For example, assume I have two files, one named kiwi.txt that contains the text "Kiwis are small, brown, and fuzzy", and another file called food.txt that holds the text "They are good to eat." Let's see what happens when I cat them.

```
>cat kiwi.txt food.txt

Kiwis are small, brown, and fuzzy.
They are good to eat.
```

The contents of the two files are displayed onscreen, one after the other. Pretty easy, huh? The biggest problem you'll have with cat is that files will scroll off the screen if they are too large, but you're about to learn a way around that.

 Linux Shortcut If you want to display all the files ending in TXT in the directory, you can use wildcards with any of the commands discussed in this lesson. The command cat *.txt shows everything in the current directory that ends with TXT.

VIEWING A PAGE AT A TIME: more AND less

The cat command is fine when you want to quickly show some information—but what about large files that scroll past a bit too quickly to read? Luckily, there are some utilities specifically created for reading files from the command line: less and more. These are often referred to by the generic term *pagers*, because they display files to your window or screen one *page* at a time.

USING more

Like cat, to use more all you need to do is type the command followed by the file or files you want to display.

For example

```
>more longfile.txt
```

This displays the file longfile.txt using more. Showing the output of the command would be a waste of space, because the results are simply the contents of the file, shown one page at a time. Instead, here are some commands you can use from within more to control the process.

- **Spacebar**—Advances the output to the next page.

- **q**—Quits the more program, exiting to the command line.

- **s**— Skips forward one line in the file. Use this to slowly advance through the file.

- **f**—Skips an entire page in the file.

- **/<pattern>**—Searches and jumps to a pattern or word in the file.

- **b**—Scrolls back one page in the file.

- **? or h**—Displays help for the more command. Because you can use this while viewing a file, it's probably the most important one to remember.

more should be available on any Linux or UNIX computer that you to use. If you're lucky, your system might include (and most modern Linux distributions do) less. Believe it or not, less is more than more.

USING less

less is a more modern pager than more, one of its main features is the capability to move around within files with less difficulty than more. Again, invoking less is identical to using cat and more; supply the files you want to view as arguments to the command.

For example

```
>less longfile.txt
```

As with more, less will display longfile.txt a page at a time. Controlling less's output is similar to more. There are several commands that allow you to move around within less.

- **Spacebar**—Advances the output to the next page.

- **b**—Backs up one page.

- **q**—Quits out of the less program, exiting to the command line.

- **Up arrow**—Scrolls up one line.

- **Down arrow**—Scrolls down one line.

- **/<pattern>**—Searches and jumps to a pattern or word in the file. This search is performed from the current point in the file to the bottom of the file.

- **?<pattern>**—Searches backward and jumps to a pattern or word in the file.

- **h**—Displays help for the less command.

Please keep in mind that this is not meant to be a comprehensive list of all the options that more and less support. In fact, if I were to write about all the options you can use with less, it would probably occupy 20 pages. This is meant to give you enough information to get started. Exploring is half the fun of using Linux!

PEEKING AT PARTS OF A FILE: head AND tail

There are some instances when you're only interested in what is stored at the top or bottom of a file. (Really, it isn't as crazy as it sounds!) Suppose you have a directory filled with saved email or newsgroup messages. Rather than displaying each message in its entirety, you might just want to see the header of the file, which contains the subject and sender address. To do this, you use the head command. Similarly, if you're running a Web server and want to see the last few people who accessed your site, you can use tail to look at the end of your log file.

USING head

You should be noticing a common thread between all the programs we've looked at. To run them, all you need to do is supply the command followed by the file or files you want to view. The same holds true for head. By default, head displays the first 10 lines of each file you specify.

For example

```
>head news112.msg
```

```
From ksteinmetz@nwu.edu Mon Mar   4 13:11:12 PST 1998
Article: 28223 of comp.sys.next.sysadmin
Path: magnus.acs.ohio-state.edu!math.ohio-state.edu!newsfeed
➥.acns.nwu.edu!news.acns.nwu.edu!news
From: ksteinmetz@nwu.edu (Kimberly A. Steinmetz)
Newsgroups: comp.sys.next.sysadmin
Subject: Re: Q: Booting lockup? How to solve?
Date: 3 Mar 1996 18:23:32 GMT
Organization: Northwestern University, Evanston, IL, US
Lines: 44
Message-ID: <4hco34$o26@news.acns.nwu.edu>
```

In this example, the first 10 lines of the file news112.msg are displayed. If you want to change the number of lines that are displayed, use the option -n, where n is the number of lines you want to see.

USING `tail`

`tail` is the inverse of `head`. Instead of displaying files from the start of a file, `tail` shows what is at the end of a file. Because most logs grow by adding things to the end, `tail` is a very nice way to see the latest additions to any log.

For example

```
>tail /var/log/httpd/access_log
```

```
204.123.9.20 - - [28/Nov/1998:00:52:40 -0500] "GET /lifetime
➥/lt2-1e.html HTTP/1.0" 200 3398
204.123.9.20 - - [28/Nov/1998:00:52:40 -0500] "GET /lifetime
➥/lt1-2a.html HTTP/1.0" 200 3561
204.123.9.20 - - [28/Nov/1998:00:52:41 -0500] "GET /enviro/
➥fa97/enviro_5.html HTTP/1.0" 200 3839
204.123.9.20 - - [28/Nov/1998:00:52:41 -0500] "GET /enviro/
➥fa97/enviro_4.html HTTP/1.0" 200 3972
204.123.9.20 - - [28/Nov/1998:00:52:42 -0500] "GET /b865/
➥b865_01.html HTTP/1.0" 200 15368
204.123.9.20 - - [28/Nov/1998:00:52:42 -0500] "GET /agf-fact
➥/agf-125.html HTTP/1.0" 200 13540
204.123.9.20 - - [28/Nov/1998:00:52:43 -0500] "GET /aex-fact
➥/463.html HTTP/1.0" 404 170
204.123.9.20 - - [28/Nov/1998:00:52:43 -0500] "GET /aex-fact
➥/480_76.html HTTP/1.0" 404 173
204.123.9.20 - - [28/Nov/1998:00:52:43 -0500] "GET /hyg-fact/
➥3000/3019.html HTTP/1.0" 200 8127
216.106.18.176 - - [28/Nov/1998:00:52:55 -0500] "GET / HTTP/
➥1.1" 200 15679
```

The last 10 entries from my Web server log are displayed. Because the log file is around 50MB in size, it's a good thing I don't have to read through it with cat or more just to see what's at the bottom! You can change the number of lines that tail displays by adding the -<*number of lines*>l option.

An extremely useful feature of tail is the capability to show files as they grow, rather than just showing the end of a file and exiting. Using the -f (follow) option with tail opens a file, displays the last 10 lines, and starts monitoring the file for new information. When a new line of data is written to the file, it is immediately displayed onscreen. To interactively monitor the Web server log from the previous example, I could use tail -f /var/log/httpd/access_log to see hits on my Web server as they occur. Pressing **Ctrl+c** exits this tail mode.

OTHER FILE FORMATS

Besides text files, you might encounter other documentation and README file formats on your Linux computer that you need to look at. Here is a brief summary.

- **GZ**—This is a gzipped (compressed) file. Some documentation might be stored in this format. Rather than ungzipping the file, you can use zcat to display the file directly.

- **PS, EPS**—These are PostScript files. If you look at these files, you'll notice that you can read the contents, but there is a lot of extraneous formatting information. Check out the ghostscript (or gs) command if you need to view a PostScript file.

- **HTML**—Obviously, HTML files. If you aren't running the X Window System, you can read HTML files from the command line with the Lynx Web browser.

- **TEX**—A TeX formatted file. TeX is a page layout language that is sometimes used to store program documentation. Look to the tex utility to work with these files.

That should cover most of the cases that you'll encounter. Luckily, most everything readable in Linux is stored as an HTML or text file. You'll probably never need to worry about other formats.

SUMMARY

Your Linux computer is filled with tons of documentation and HOWTO files. Unfortunately, a HOWTO on how to read files isn't going to do you much good. This lesson gives you a clear picture of the many different ways you can display files or portions of files. Following is a review of some of the key points from this lesson:

- **cat**—The concatenate command displays all the files you specify, one after the other. It does not pause at the end of pages.

- **more/less**—more and less are known as pagers. They page through their input files, one screen at a time. less offers the capability to scroll backward through files, unlike more, which provides forward-only viewing.

- **head**—Displays the first few lines of a file. This is useful when you're trying to look at header information in files such as email messages.

- **tail**—Views the end of a file. Used with the -f option, tail provides the capability of displaying a logfile as it is generated. Rather than each program needing its own monitoring utility, tail -f can be used instead.

- **Other file formats**—Although most Linux information files are text- or HTML-based, there are other formats that you might encounter. This lesson looks briefly at some of those formats, and the programs that you can use to work with them.

LESSON 8
TEXT EDITING

In this lesson, you will learn the basics of editing files in the Linux environment.

Many Linux programs use text files as input, create text files as output, or are configured commands and variables set up in a text file. In order to change the contents of these files you need to use a text editor.

As a matter of fact, most Linux software doesn't know the difference between a text file and any other file. From the operating system's point of view, files are files are files. If the user chooses to view some of them as containing text, and others as containing programs, that's the user's business. An interesting consequence of this lack of concern over a file's contents is that the operating system is just as happy to let you use a text editor to edit the contents of your spreadsheet program as it is to let you attempt to run your email. Of course, if you actually have execute permission set on your email and try to run it, it's almost certain to segmentation-fault (crash) immediately, but Linux *will* try.

 Editing to Your Advantage   If you are a programmer you might find this lack of a distinction to be useful. On occasion, you might find a program that needs a minor change, such as correction of a misspelling or a change of wording. In this instance, it is sometimes most convenient to load the executable file into a text editor and make the correction directly in the binary. This isn't a trick for the faint of heart, but sometimes, it's the quick fix you need...and sometimes it's the only fix for software that you don't have the source code for.

If you spend much time discussing Linux editors with long-time Linux users, you'll find that there is a disagreement of warlike proportions between the users of the two most common editors—vi and emacs. While these editors are actually rather complementary in their functions and are both useful tools to have in your toolbox, chances are you'll end up running into many users who insist that one or the other is completely useless. If you listen to them, you'll be depriving yourself of the better solution to at least some tasks.

Most Linux editors have immense power. emacs, for example, contains not only its own built-in programming language, but also can function as a complete windowing system for users who are stuck on text-only terminals. However, there is not enough room in this quick guide to cover more than the basics. After mastering the simple tasks presented here, the interested reader should make a trip to the library or bookstore and choose from among the several books available on each of the more popular Linux editors.

QUICK AND DIRTY EDITING: vi

The vi editor is Linux's most universal editor. Some users pronounce it *vee-eye*; others pronounce it *vye*. (There seems to be no consensus, but the people who call it *vye* are still wrong!) vi isn't an easy editor, and it isn't a friendly editor. What it is, however, is a quick-starting editor with a very small memory footprint that you will find on every Linux machine that you use. Because of its ubiquity, knowing the basics of vi allows you to work with your files even if no more-convenient editors are available.

If you need to use vi, you should

1. Determine what file you want to edit.

2. Issue the vi command as **vi <filename>**. The vi editor can also be started with no filename if you prefer to start a new document but haven't decided on a name.

After you start vi, there are a number of things you need to know to make it useful.

vi operates in one of two modes: Command mode and Insert mode. In

Command mode, you have control of things such as cursor position, deleting characters, and saving files. In Insert mode, you can insert characters. This distinction is bound to be confusing at first, but you'll find that vi's speed and universal presence outweigh its odd interface when performing some tasks. Some of the most used tasks are featured in Table 8.1.

TABLE 8.1   COMMON vi ACTIONS

MODE	KEY(S)/KEY COMBINATION(S)	ACTION
Command	l	Move right
	h	Move left
	j	Move to the next line
	k	Move to the previous line
	Put cursor on the character to delete, and then press the x key	Delete a character
	Press the d key twice	Delete an entire line (including to delete an empty line)
	Position cursor on the line append and hit A	Append the to end of a line
	i (before the character under the cursor) or a (after the character under the cursor)	Changes to Insert mode
	:w+Return	Save the file
	:w<filename>	Save the file with a new name

continues

TABLE 8.1   COMMON vi ACTIONS

MODE	KEY(S)/KEY COMBINATION(S)	ACTION
	:q+Return	To exit vi
	:q!+Return	Quit without saving
Insert	Esc key	Changes to Command mode
	Backspace and Delete keys	Backspaces or deletes, but only for data just inserted

Because it would be impossible to walk through a step-by-step example, you should try typing the following example—remember to compare what you're typing, refer to the commands in Table 8.1, and see what happens. While the finer details will not be revealed by this example, you should pick up enough to at least get useful work done and get you out of any sticky vi situations you happen to get into.

Type the following exactly as it appears. Where a new line appears in the text, press **Return**. Remember that **Esc** is the Escape key.

```
> vi mynewfile
iThis is my new file
This is line one of my new file
This is a test
This is line four of my new file<esc>kddkA
This is line three of my new file<esc>khhhhhhhhhhhhhhhhhh
xxxitwo<esc>:wq!
```

Your machine should respond

```
"mynewfile" [New file] 4 lines, 119 characters
```

Now, look at what you've got.

```
> cat mynewfile

This is my new file
This is line two of my new file
```

```
This is line three of my new file
This is line four of my new file
```

THE KING OF EDITORS: emacs

On the other end of the spectrum from `vi`'s odd syntax and tiny footprint is emacs. In certain circles it is thought that emacs is an acronym for "emacs makes a computer slow," as emacs is certainly the editor of all editors. Including an email-reading client, a news-reading client, a programming language, an online Help database, and a windowing system, to name only a few of its features, emacs can almost certainly do anything that you want an editor to do. With today's faster machines and almost unlimited memory, emacs might even be capable of doing its job fast enough that you don't need a coffee break while it starts up.

From the point of view of the average user, emacs has a much more intuitive interface than `vi`. You're always in Insert mode, and control functions are handled by using control-key sequences instead of a separate mode. To make use of emacs, you need to

1. Determine the name of the file you want to edit.

2. Issue the emacs command as **emacs <filename>**. The emacs editor can also be started without a filename if you want to create a new file.

After you've started emacs, you'll need to know some basics to make it useful. In the following list, whenever you see **Ctrl** preceding a character, it means that you should hold down the **Ctrl** key and type that character. You hardly need the list that follows because emacs starts up by immediately giving you a list of ways to get help.

- The emacs editor doesn't have a separate mode for entering commands. You are always either typing a command or typing text—no switching modes between them. This is just like most word processors you are familiar with. To enter text, type what you want to appear. To enter a command, press the command (usually **Ctrl+someletter**, or **Esc+x** *somecommand*).

- You can position the cursor keys in emacs by using the arrow-key keypad and terminal combination in most every version of emacs. If the arrow keys don't work, you can also position the cursor by using **Ctrl+f** to move forward, **Ctrl+b** to move backward, **Ctrl+p** to move to the previous line, and **Ctrl+n** to move to the next line. Newer versions of emacs also allow you to position the cursor using the mouse, but many users actually find this less convenient than the cursor keys.

- You can delete everything from the cursor to the end of the current line by pressing **Ctrl+k**.

- **Ctrl+g** is emacs' "quit what you're doing" command—if you've started pressing a command and change your mind, use **Ctrl+g**.

- If you use **Ctrl+k** to delete a line or lines, you can press **Ctrl+y** to "yank" them back again.

- To save the file you're currently editing, press **Ctrl+x+Ctrl+s**.

- To save the file to a new filename, press **Ctrl+x+Ctrl+w<*filename*>**.

- To exit emacs, press **Ctrl+x+Ctrl+c**. If emacs proceeds to ask you about *unsaved buffers*, it's because you have unsaved work. You can either go back and save your work, or answer Yes to the Quit Anyway? question and go about your business.

COMMAND BASICS

Beyond the set of **Ctrl+** commands available in emacs, there's also an amazingly extensible set of commands that come into play if you use the **Esc** key. These commands are usually known as emacs *Meta commands*, though the machine with the Meta key from which they draw their name has long since faded into history. While they're too complicated and too specific to cover in this book, access to many of the interesting emacs Meta commands is accomplished by pressing **Esc+x**, and then pressing a command of some sort, such as *info,* *what-line*, or *goto-line*. As a matter of fact, you can find many useful emacs commands by entering **Esc+x,** and then typing a few characters of the beginning of what you think the command might be named, followed by a space. The editor then gives you a list of all commands with similar names—frequently one that does what you want is on the list!

One useful Meta command that you might want to try is to start emacs, and type `Esc+xhelp+Spacebar` (and a second space, if the first one just results in the `help` you typed being extended by a dash). This brings up a list of emacs commands that start with *Help*—including useful things such as Help for Help, a very good place to start.

THE EMACS TUTORIAL

Instead of a quick sample for you to go through, emacs provides its own help and tutorial functions. New users are always encouraged to take the emacs tutorial to introduce themselves to the features of the editor and to learn how to ask it for help with other features.

To enter the emacs tutorial, start emacs and type **Ctrl+hi** (hold the **Ctrl** key down, press **h**, release the Ctrl key, and press **i**). If you type a **?** after the **Ctrl+h** instead of the **i**, you'll see that there's actually a whole world of alternatives to the **i**, which give you a large range of different types of helpful information. For now, take the tutorial. If you're curious, you can probably spend a few months exploring the other options.

KDE'S BUILT-IN EDITOR

KDE provides a very convenient point-and-click text editor with all the convenient mouse-based functionality you have probably come to expect from personal computer editing programs.

To activate the KDE editor, click the **K** in the KDE toolbar. Now, choose **Applications** from the pop-up menu and then **Editor** from its submenu. A window that looks like the one shown in Figure 8.1 will open.

FIGURE 8.1   The KDE has an easy-to-use, built-in editor.

Editor Patience   Sometimes it takes a few seconds to for X Windows-based applications to start—and there's no spinning watch cursor to let you know the machine is actually doing what you asked it to. Don't worry if the editor doesn't open immediately. If you select the editor again before it opens, you'll eventually end up with two editors running.

The built-in KDE editor includes all the normal point-and-click select, copy, insert, and delete features you would expect from a GUI-based editor. In addition, it uses KDE's data-location abstraction, so you can open files directly from an FTP or Web site using its URL. In Figure 8.1, you can see one of the KDE text editor menus is selected. Several of these convenient features are visible on the drop-down menu that has appeared.

SUMMARY

In this lesson, you were introduced to the two most popular text editors on the Linux platform: vi and emacs. It is best with both of these editors to learn by doing, and this lesson provides you with the tools necessary to do the three most important tasks in a text editor: start the editor, edit text, and exit gracefully if you mess up. Because you know how to quit without saving from both vi and emacs, don't be afraid to experiment. You also learned about KDE's built-in editor as a desktop environment alternative to the text window-based editors from the older Linux world. Let's review:

- **The vi editor is fast and convenient for making small changes to files**—It has a user interface that is nonintuitive at the kindest. The omnipresence of the vi editor, its speed of execution, and small disk-space requirements make it a convenient choice for fast edits, and for when you're at an unfamiliar machine.

- **Esc+q!**—Gets you out of vi in a hurry, without saving any changes.

- **The emacs editor contains everything you need in an editor, and then some, and then some more**—On older hardware, emacs was a very slow to start, very slow to respond editor, but this has been largely mitigated by today's fast machines and extremely inexpensive disk space and memory. Take the emacs tutorial, dig around in its information files (**Esc+xinfo+Return**) and find a book on emacs to read if you want to get the most out of this editor.

- **Ctrl+x+Ctrl+c**—Followed by answering Yes to any Quit Anyway? questions gets you out of emacs in a hurry, without saving any changes you've made.

LESSON 9

OTHER TEXT AND FILE UTILITIES

In this lesson you'll round out your look at text utilities by learning how to perform some routine and not-so-routine tasks on text files.

Some of what you're going to see in this lesson might not seem to be useful, but used in conjunction with other commands it can be very powerful. If you take up shell scripting, which is discussed in Lesson 14, "Basic Shell Scripting," you'll appreciate that Linux includes utilities that make your programming life simpler.

COUNTING LINES, WORDS, AND CHARACTERS: wc

If you'd like to get quick statistics about a text file on your machine, but don't want to load it into a word processor, you can use the wc command to provide information on the number of lines, words, and characters within a single file.

To use wc, supply the name of a file you want analyzed, in the form **wc** **<filename>**. If you pass more than one filename to wc, all the files will be processed, and a grand total for everything will also be returned.

For example

```
>wc *.txt

    300    2799    16284 intro.txt
   4944   43494   257939 lesson7.txt
   5244   46293   274223 total
```

In this example, wc has processed all the TXT files in the current directory (intro.txt and lesson7.txt). Four columns of information are returned for each file. The first value is the number of lines in the file, the second is a count of the words in the file, and the third is the number of characters. The final column, of course, is the filename. If you want to limit the values to lines, words, or characters, you can use the -l, -w, or -c options respectively.

Uses for wc   A common use I have for wc is to check the number of entries in my log files. For example, to see how many "hits" my Web server has received since the last time the log files were reset, I use a command such as wc -l /var/log/httpd/access_log. This returns the number of lines in my access_log file. Because each line represents a hit, I can use wc to quickly count the hits.

SORTING INFORMATION: sort

Sorting is another useful function that you can do quickly with a built-in command, instead of writing a specialized utility to do it. For example, suppose I have a file called kiwi.txt that contains the following:

```
Joan   92
Will   78
John   21
Kim    99
Kama   05
Jack   07
```

It's pretty simple to sort these by hand (ignoring the numbers for now), but what if you have several thousand names, instead of six? Then you can use the sort command. Let's try running sort on kiwi.txt to see what happens:

```
>sort kiwi.txt
```

```
Jack   07
Joan   92
John   21
```

```
Kama   05
Kim    99
Will   78
```

Everything is sorted as you would expect. Now, what if, instead of wanting to sort by the name, you want to sort by the number? To do this, you'd need to follow these steps:

1. Figure out what column you want to sort by; you'll inform sort of your decision by using +*<columnnumber>* as an argument to the command.

2. You also need to tell sort what character is separating the columns using the -t option. In this case it's a few spaces, so use -t" ".

3. Lastly, because there are a varying number of spaces between the name and number, you'll need to use ignore blanks option -b to tell sort to count a group of spaces as a single space.

For example

```
>sort +2 -t" " -b kiwi.txt
```

```
Kama   05
Jack   07
John   21
Will   78
Joan   92
Kim    99
```

Bingo! It's exactly what you were hoping for, right? Now the file is sorted by the numbers in the second column. sort has many more options that you can explore on your own with the man pages, but you should see how it can be used to sort a variety of data stored in different formats.

CHOPPING UP FILES: split

Suppose you need to email a huge file to a friend, but his or her email system doesn't support receiving messages as large as you'd like. Time to write a special splitting utility? Nope, it's already been done for you. The split command can cut up a file into whatever length segments you'd like, based on the number of lines in a file or the bytes. To use split

1. Choose your input file. For this example, I'm using kiwi.txt from the sort command.

2. Determine the number of lines you want stored in each output file. You'll specify this with **-l** *<number of lines>* as an option to the sort command. If you prefer to use the number of K or MB, you can do use the -b option with k or m. For example, -l 3 divides a file into segments of three lines each. Using -b 10k results in segments 10K in size. Lastly, -b 10m creates 10MB segments.

3. Choose a base output filename for the results.

4. Invoke sort using the syntax **split** *<segmentoptions>* *<inputfile>* *<outputfile>*

For example

```
>split -l 3 kiwi.txt kiwisplit
>more kiwisplit*

::::::::::::::
kiwisplitaa
::::::::::::::
Joan   92
Will   78
John   21
::::::::::::::
kiwisplitab
::::::::::::::
Kim    99
Kama   05
Jack   07
```

The kiwi.txt file from the previous example has been run through split and divided into two files of three lines each: kiwisplitaa and kiwisplitab. I've displayed the contents of the files using the more command, because split does not offer feedback on completion.

After your files are split to a reasonable size, you can transmit them to the pesky mail server, or whatever else you'd like. This is just another example of a built-in utility that will undoubtedly come in handy when you least expect it.

To reassemble the files, use the `cat` command like this: `cat <filename>*`
`> <fullfile>`. This will take all the files with the base name `filename`
and stick them back together in fullfile.

> **Working with Output Files**   It's frequently best to call
> output files things such as `complete.file`—something
> completely different than the `<basename>`, and then
> move them to their destination or final filename. This
> avoids potential confusion in those cases where you'd
> really like your final filename to be just `<basename>`.

DIFFERENCES AND PATCHES: `diff` AND `patch`

Something that you might be accustomed to is creating documents and
sending out revisions. Unfortunately, most of the time you probably have
to send out entire copies of new files when only a few words here and
there have changed. In the Linux community, there is a great deal of
information exchange, and source code is passed back and forth constantly. Rather than always sending complete files, people reply on the
`diff` and `patch` commands to transfer only whatever information has
changed between files.

USING `diff`

The `diff` function takes two files, an original template file and an updated
file, and produces an output patch file that contains enough information to
reconstruct the updated file given only the patch file and the template file.
Assume I have the original file templatefile.txt, which has the contents:

```
Now is the time for all good
kiwis to come to the aid of
puppies.
```

I've distributed this file amongst all my coworkers. (This is just an example folks!) However, a few days later, I updated my file to a new file
called updatedfile.txt, which looks like this:

```
Now is the time for all good and bad
kiwis to come to the aid of
puppies and children.
```

Rather than redistribute the new file updatedfile.txt to everyone, I can make a patch that contains all the changes between the original and the new file. To do this, I use the `diff` command with the following syntax: **diff <template file> <updated file> > <patch file>**. The patch file can have any filename you'd like.

Redirecting Output   The standalone > in this example is used to redirect output to a specific file, which you name. You'll learn more about this in Lesson 12, "Input and Output."

For example

```
>diff templatefile.txt updatedfile.txt > patchfile.txt
```

The program will run and return a command line with no messages. If you're interested in seeing what the patch file contains, feel free to take a look at it with `cat` or `more`. In this example, the resulting patch file is named patchfile.txt—you should distribute it to everyone who has the original templatefile.txt and who needs to update it.

File Comparisons   The `diff` command is also useful when you want to know if two copies of the same file are identical or not. If you find yourself with multiple copies of similar files, `diff` is a fast way to find out whether they are identical, and if not, what changes have been made between them. If `diff` produces no output, there are no differences between the files.

USING patch

Now, the patch program comes into play. You invoke patch by giving it the name of the file to patch, followed by the name of the patch file.

For example

```
>patch templatefile.txt patchfile.txt
```

```
patching file `templatefile.txt'
```

That's all there is to it. The file templatefile.txt has now been updated and is identical to the updatedfile.txt file. You can verify this by viewing templatefile.txt.

```
>cat templatefile.txt
```

```
Now is the time for all good and bad
kiwis to come to the aid of
puppies and children.
```

Yep! Pretty nifty. If you looked at the patch file, you might have noticed that it is about the same size as updatedfile.txt, so why not just distribute the entire file instead of the patch? In the case of tiny files like those used in this example, it really doesn't make sense to create patches. If you're dealing with files several thousand lines long that have one or two lines changed somewhere in the middle, you'll find that patch and diff are excellent ways to avoid sending gobs of redundant information.

Important Reminder   Always remember to keep a copy of your template file. In this example, I applied the patch to my template file, and my template file has now been updated. If all further patches are created from the updated file, no problem; I'm ready to go. However, if patches are created based on the original template, my templatefile.txt will no longer be capable of being patched.

SUMMARY

I hope you found this lesson interesting. The commands you've learned should show you a bit of the power that is built into the Linux operating system. You've probably seen utilities like this before on other desktop systems, but they've been add-ons or pieces of commercial software. In the case of Linux, it's all free, and there's a whole lot more where this stuff came from! Let's review what is discussed in this lesson:

- **wc**—The wc command can provide quick character, line, and word counts for a single file or group of files.

- **sort**—Sort enables you to sort information sorted on separate lines within a text file. It understands the notion of columns and fields of data, so you can use it to sort data in a variety of different formats.

- **split**—If you have files that are a bit too large to handle when sending email, writing to a floppy, and so on, you can use the split command to chop them up into smaller files. split can create files containing a certain number of lines, kilobytes, or megabytes.

- **diff/patch**—The combination of diff and patch enables you to distribute updates to documents, source code, and so on, in an efficient manner. Rather than sending entire copies of updated files, you can use diff to create patch files that only contain the changes between one version of a file and the next.

LESSON 10

COMPRESSION AND ARCHIVING TOOLS

In this lesson you will learn about the common Linux tools for compressing and archiving files. You will also learn about a few tools you can use to keep tabs on your disk usage.

While conserving disk space has almost become a thing of the past, it is still occasionally necessary to compress your files, or bundle them up for archival purposes.

COMPRESSING FILES

Historically, hard-disk storage space has been an expensive commodity, in both the corporate and home-use environments.

Times Sure Do Change On a purely historical note, an 80MB SCSI-1 drive cost $369 in 1988, and a 20MB MFM replacement drive for a PC-AT recently found by a friend of the author included its original packing receipt—a bill to the tune of $720! Today, $500 can buy 5GB or more of storage!

With today's extremely inexpensive hard drives, the pressure to maximize disk usage efficiency is much lower than it has been in the past, but in some environments such as schools, the pressure is still present. If you happen to be using a system where disk space is at a premium, you can use the commands in the compression section of this lesson to reduce the amount of space your files occupy, or to fit more stuff in the space you are allowed. Even if disk space isn't a concern for you, there are occasions, such as when sending files around via email or distributing them over the Internet, when compressing files might be a wise choice.

There are three major compression formats you are likely to encounter when using Linux: *compressed* files made using the Linux program compress, *zipped* files made using Linux or PC versions of the PKZip program, and *gzipped* files made using the GNU gzip utility. Each of these formats has a set of programs for compressing and uncompressing files. Also appearing recently is the *bzip2* compression utility, which, while fairly new, looks very promising for tight compression.

USING compress/uncompress/zcat

The creatively named compress command uses an older UNIX compression format that is slowly dying out as the gzip format gains popularity. Files created with the compress command have the file suffix Z. To use the compress command to compress a file, issue the command as **compress <filename>**.

The equally creatively named uncompress command uncompresses (surprise!) the results of a compress command. To use the uncompress command, issue the command as **uncompress <filename.Z>**

The zcat command (with its slightly less intuitive name) is a version of cat that reads compressed files rather than normal text files.

Using zcat is as intuitive as compress and uncompress **zcat <filename.Z>**. To make zcat somewhat more useful if it's a large file you're trying to look at, you can *pipe* the output into your pager of preference. To do this, issue the command as **zcat <filename.Z> ¦ more**. The vertical bar, ¦, is the Linux pipe character—it pipes the output of the command preceding it into the input of the command following it. (You'll learn more about this in Lesson 12, "Input and Output.")

For example, if you have a compressed file named stuffed.Z, and you want to read it without bothering to uncompress it first, you can type

```
> zcat stuffed.Z ¦ more
```

Your machine should respond by using more to page you through the document.

USING `zip/unzip`

Based on the algorithm from the PC standard PKZip program, the zip and unzip programs work exactly as you would expect them to: **zip** **<*filename*>** to compress a file with zip, and **unzip** **<*filename.z*>** to unzip the files.

Creating files using the zip format (which uses the file suffix Z in Linux) for distribution to other Linux users is generally not a good idea, as zip and unzip are not always available to Linux users. (These utilities are freeware—get your system administrator to install them if you need to have access to them.) If your target, however, is Macintosh or Windows users, zip is a format that they should be able to read.

Both the zip and unzip programs have a number of potentially useful options, a list of which can be displayed by issuing either command followed by the option -h.

USING `gzip/gunzip`

The GNU gzip suite was created in response to the realization that Linux's compress/uncompress programs were based on proprietary algorithms and that this might someday entail licensing fees. Again, the gzip/gunzip programs work essentially identically to the compress/uncompress/zcat suite. Files compressed in the gzip format use the file suffix GZ, and are generally smaller than files compressed with compress. If you'd like, you can use these commands to work with Z (compress) files.

What's this BZ2 File? There is a new compression format that has a slightly better compression ratio than gzip; these are identified by the BZ2 extension. The commands to work with these files are bzip2 and unbzip2. The syntax is nearly identical to gzip/gunzip, so you shouldn't have any problem dealing with them.

bzip2/bunzip2

While a relatively new addition to the Linux/UNIX compression scene, the bzip2 compressor appears to produce better compression than either compress or gzip. The syntax and options for bzip2 have intentionally been made similar to gzip, so if you should encounter this program as it grows in popularity, you shouldn't have too much trouble figuring it out. Compression with bzip2 follows the gzip format of: **bzip2 <*filename*>**, which produces the compressed file **<*filename*.bz2>**. Decompression is simply **bunzip2 <*filename*.bz2>**.

The bzip2 compression and decompression utilities appear to be in development as of this writing, so it would not be surprising to find that the commands evolve over time (bzip2 and .bz2 files are an update of a prior bzip program that made BZ files). If you encounter these programs and need to do more than trivial compressions or decompressions, it is recommended that you consult your local man pages for more current information.

MANAGING YOUR DISK USAGE

If you're on a system where you need to worry about disk usage, have a disk quota that you must remain under, or are just curious about how much space your files are taking up, there are a number of commands you can use to look at this data:

- **ls**—Turning back to Lesson 4, "The File System," you can use the ls command with the -l option to display disk usage for a file or files. If you need to scan quickly through your files to see which ones are taking up the most room, this is a quick way to do it.

- **find**—In Lesson 5, "Finding Files," you were introduced to using the find command to find files over a certain size. While similar in utility to the ls -l command for this purpose, find -size # is a faster way to collect information on all files over # kilobytes—you just have to know what # you're looking for.

- **df**—Used mostly by system administrators, the df command provides information about disk usage. Depending on your version of Linux, you might have to give df different options to get it to produce readable output, but the general form you'd be interested in is df . /, which asks the file system to tell you about the usage of the drive that the current directory resides on. The response will usually be in the form of a logical device name that you can ignore, followed by information about the total capacity of the device, the amount of storage in use on the device, the percentage of usage of the device, and the *mount point* (path to the directory at which the device appears) for the device. You might have to try variations on df . / or df -k . /, or check your man pages to find the option that works on your version of Linux.

- **du**—Another system administrator type command, du provides information about disk usage by directory. Again, different versions of Linux use slightly different syntaxes, but the general form you will be most interested in is du -s *, which asks the file system to produce a disk usage summary for everything in the current directory. For each item in the current directory du -s * will return a summary of the total disk space used by the contents of the files or directories. Depending on your version of Linux, you might or might not need to supply du with the -k flag to convince it to show you the disk usage in values of kilobytes (otherwise it shows you the disk usage in values of the file system's native block-size—usually 512 bytes).

ARCHIVING FILES: tar

If you spend much time using Linux systems, you're bound to run into tar files. *Tar* is short for tape archive, though the tar command and its output are very rarely used for archiving to tape anymore. More sophisticated and more powerful programs have taken over the job of archiving to tape, but the tar command remains a convenient and useful tool for personal archiving and distribution of files.

The tar command, in its simplest form, either creates or unpacks archive files. When creating an archive, you provide tar with a filename for the archive and a list of files to archive. The program then collects all the files and bundles them into a single tar file, which you can then store for future use or distribute conveniently via the World Wide Web, FTP, or email. When unpacking archives, you provide `tar` with the name of a tar file, and it extracts the contents of the file into the current directory, with the exact same filenames, paths, and contents that existed on the system where it was tarred.

To use `tar` to create an archive

1. Determine the name you want for your archive tar file—normally it should have the suffix TAR.

2. Determine the filenames of all the files you'd like to include in the `tar` file, or, more normally, the name of a directory that you'd like to archive the contents of.

3. Issue the `tar` command as **tar -cvf <*tarfilename*.tar> <*files or directories*>**

For example, if you have a directory named lots-a-stuff in the current directory, you could archive the entire contents of lots-a-stuff (all the files, all the directories, and all the files in all the directories, and so on) by typing

```
> tar -cvf lotsastuff.tar lots-a-stuff
```

Your machine would respond (because you gave it the -v, or verbose option) by telling you about every file that it's putting in the archive, and in the end you would have a new file named lotsastuff.tar. This new file would contain the entire contents of your lots-a-stuff directory, with all the directory structure and file attribute information intact.

To unpack a tar file, issue the command **tar -xvf <*tarfilename*.tar>**.

If you gave this file to a friend, your friend could then unpack the tar file by typing

```
> tar -xvf lotsastuff.tar
```

After a list of everything in the file (that -v option again) your friend would have a new directory named lots-a-stuff in his or her current directory, and it would contain the complete contents of your lots-a-stuff directory. Any subdirectories in your lots-a-stuff directory would be present, as well as all their contents.

Polite Use of `tar`   If you don't know what is in a tar file, it's a good idea to use `tar -tvf <tarfile.tar>` before unpacking it. The `-t` option is the `tell` option and asks `tar` to tell you about the contents of the file rather than unpacking it. This is a useful way to determine if the person who created the tar file was a nice person who put everything in a directory, and then tarred the directory; or if he or she was an impolite person who did not put everything in the current directory before tarring it. If you run into a tar file created by an impolite user, and make the mistake of untarring it in an inconvenient place—your home directory, for example—tar will end up dribbling files all over your home directory. You will then be stuck finding all the files and putting them in a subdirectory by hand, sometimes a very tedious process. Be a polite user—don't `tar` files; `tar` directories.

PREPARING FOR EMAIL
TRANSMISSION: uuencode/uudecode

If you need to send your files to another user, you can do this easily by including them in an email message. PINE, for example, lets you attach a file by pressing **Ctrl+J**. If you don't have PINE on your system, you can use the oldest encoding standard available, uuencode. This lets you encode files for transmission even on the most basic Linux installations. The uuencode program accepts any file as input, and it produces an encoding of the file that can be included in an email message. The contents of this file look like random characters, but on the receiving end, the user can use the uudecode program to extract the original file. Because every email program is different, you'll need to consult the documentation for your email client on how to include a file into a message. Here you'll just learn how to create the uuencoded file from your original, and how to uudecode it again on the other side.

To use the uuencode command

1. Determine the name of the file you want to encode for email transmission.

2. Determine what you'd like the file to call itself at the other end.

3. Issue the uuencode command as **uuencode <*filename*>** **<*callmethis*> > <*filename*>.uue** (yes, you need to type the > before the <*filename*>.uue argument).

Your computer should then produce a file named <*filename*>.uue which contains the uuencoded version of the file.

For example, if you have a file named sendtojoe, and you'd want to uuencode it, you could type

```
> uuencode sendtojoe hijoe > joe.uue
```

Your computer would produce a file named joe.uue, which when decoded by Joe would be named hijoe, and would contain the contents of your sendtojoe file.

Now you can copy and paste, include, or do whatever you need to do to insert the file you just created into an email message, and send it wherever you like.

Of course, if you receive a uuencoded file, you will need to know how to decode the file. Decoding a uuencoded file is extremely simple—issue the uudecode command as **uudecode <*filename.uue*>.**

Your machine should produce a file in the current directory identical to the one originally uuencoded.

 Clearing up UUE   The filename of the UUE file, and the filename to which it will decode itself do not have to be the same. This is sometimes confusing. If you receive a file named fuzzykiwi.uue, issue the **uudecode fuzzykiwi.uue** command, and you do not find a file named fuzzykiwi in your directory, do not be alarmed. The uuencoded file contains the filename as well as the uuencoded file contents. To find out what the uudecoded file will be named, use the head command to look at the first few lines of the uuencoded file. The filename that it will decode to appears on the first line.

KDE ARCHIVING TOOLS

Desktop environments also provide convenient drag-and-drop file compression and archiving tools. The KDE environment, for example, provides the KZip archive and compression tool.

To access the KZip tool, click the K on the KDE toolbar, choose Utilities from the pop-up menu, and Zip from its submenu. A window similar to the one shown in Figure 10.1 will appear.

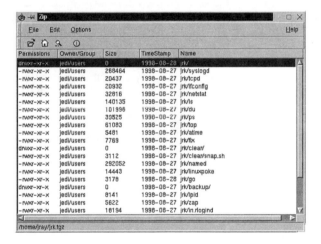

FIGURE 10.1   The KDE built-in archive manager, KZip, can graphically manage your archives.

The KDE KZip tool can work with tar and gzip files: choose Open from the File menu and select your archive. The KZip tool provides convenient features such as displaying archive entry contents by double-clicking the entry and dragging and dropping additional files to archives.

SUMMARY

When you need to conserve disk space or shorten file transmission times, you might need to resort to compacting your files with some sort of compression utility. This lesson gave you a good idea of how to use the Linux compression software. Review what you've learned:

* The three common compression utilities on Linux systems are the omnipresent compress, the newer and smarter gzip, and the cross-platform zip programs. A relatively new addition to the Linux/UNIX compression scene is bzip2, which appears to produce better compression than compress or gzip.

* When you need to provide a collection of files to other users or archive a set of files for future use, you can use tar to create tar files that contain all your files in one convenient package.

* Don't be an impolite user and use tar to archive individual files. Instead, put all the files you want to archive in a directory and tar the directory.

* If you need to send a file to someone via email, you can create an emailable encoding of the file by using the uuencode command.

* Don't be alarmed if you uudecode a file and can't immediately find it; the real filename will be stored in plain text at the beginning of the file.

LESSON 11

PROCESSES

In this lesson you will learn how to work with processes: view them, kill them, and bend them to your whims!

Everything that you've run on your system in the previous lessons, and everything that you're going to be running in the rest of the lessons, has created *processes* on your system. Each command creates a process that the Linux operating system runs until it is finished or *killed*. Unlike some desktop operating systems, you can create processes that run entirely in the background or start and run in the middle of the night without you even needing to be logged on to the computer.

MORE THAN ONE COMMAND AT A TIME

Linux allows you to run more than a single command at a time. This capability is known as *multitasking* and is available on other operating systems as well. What makes Linux different is that mundane tasks can operate in the background, even after you log out of the system.

PUTTING A COMMAND INTO THE BACKGROUND: &

Making a command run in the background is simple: add an & to the end of the line containing the command.

For example, suppose I am running a program to analyze my Web server log files called analog. Most log analysis takes quite some time for a busy Web server, so I really don't want to wait around for the command to finish. In order to run analog in the background, I could type

```
>analog /var/log/httpd/access_log &
[3] 32566
>
```

The results are a bit cryptic, but you should see that you returned to the command line, ready to go! The two numbers that are returned identify the process on the system. The first result, [3], identifies this as process number 3 that you've put in the background. The second number, 32566, is the process ID. Your Linux system potentially has hundreds of processes running on it; each one is assigned a unique number. Whatever number your process happens to be assigned will be returned as the second result value.

 Running More than One Command   To run several commands, one after the other, and put the whole group into the background, you can use this syntax: (<*command 1*>;<*command 2*>;<*command 3*>) &. This creates a new shell to execute the commands, and places it in the background. For example, if I wanted to run the analog utility on two files, I could do this: **(analog /var/log/httpd/access_log; analog /var/log/httpd/ new_access_log) &.**

SUSPENDING A COMMAND AND MOVING IT TO THE BACKGROUND: CTRL+Z AND bg

If you happen to start a command without putting it into the background, you can still turn it into a background process if you want. Let's assume I've started the analog command without the ampersand.

For example

```
>analog /var/log/httpd/access_log
```

To turn this into a background process, first press **Ctrl+z** to suspend the process.

```
<Ctrl+z>
[3]+  Stopped                    analog /var/log/httpd/access_log
```

The analog command has now been suspended, and is assigned a process number 3. Remember, this is not the same as the process ID; it identifies the process number locally in your session, not globally to the system.

To finish putting analog into the background, use the bg command followed by the local process number that you want to put into the background, as in **bg *<process number>***. In this example, analog was assigned the process number 3, so that's what I'll use in conjunction with bg.

```
>bg 3
```

```
[3]+ analog /var/log/httpd/access_log &
```

Linux responds by showing you that analog now is running with the & in the background, and you can continue using the system.

RETURNING A PROCESS TO THE FOREGROUND: fg

What happens if a process is accidentally backgrounded, or if you'd like to return a process to the foreground to manually control it or check its status? In this case, you'd use the fg command and the process number to return that process to the foreground, with the syntax **fg *<process number>***.

For example, the analog process was assigned the local process number of 3 when it was put into the background. To bring it to the foreground, type

```
>fg 3
analog /var/log/httpd/access_log
```

Now you're in complete control of the analog process again, because it is now running in the foreground.

 Missing Process Number?   What can you do if you've forgotten the local process number? Use the jobs command. The jobs command gives you a short listing of all your suspended and backgrounded processes, and their associated numbers.

LISTING THE RUNNING PROCESSES: ps

If you really start using the backgrounding capabilities of Linux, at some point you're going to want to find out what you have running. To do this, you can use the ps command. This command returns a list of all the processes that you currently own.

For example

```
>ps
  PID TTY STAT   TIME COMMAND
 8832  p1 R      0:00 ps
30674  p1 S      0:00 /bin/login -h
➥NEW93114217.columbus.here.com -p
30675  p1 S      0:00 -bash
31136  p1 T      0:00 analog /var/log/httpd/access_log
```

These are all the commands that I currently have running. The columns are the system process ID (PID), the controlling terminal, the status of the process (running, sleeping, and so on), and the process itself. These are just the processes that I own. If you'd like to see everything running, try running ps ax, which lists all the users' processes (-a) and all processes that don't have a controlling terminal (-x). The ps command has a huge number of options that can return tons of information. Take a look at the man page for more information. The primary concern right now is that you can list what you have running on the system and get your process IDs.

KILLING A PROCESS: kill, kill, kill!

Killing might sound a bit harsh for ending a process, but it does sum up the result quite nicely. When you kill a process you stop whatever it is doing, no matter what. If you're editing a file, you risk losing the entire file if you kill the process rather than exit out of it normally.

USING kill

While the command kill is mainly used to stop processes, it can also be used to send signals to a process. Depending on the signal that you send, the process might reload its configuration files and reinitialize itself. This

is extremely nice when you're running something such as a Web server
and need to add a MIME-type or something without shutting down the
server. To see a list of the signals that you can send using kill, invoke the
command with **kill -l**.

```
>kill -l
 1) SIGHUP      2) SIGINT      3) SIGQUIT     4) SIGILL
 5) SIGTRAP     6) SIGIOT      7) SIGBUS      8) SIGFPE
 9) SIGKILL    10) SIGUSR1    11) SIGSEGV    12) SIGUSR2
13) SIGPIPE    14) SIGALRM    15) SIGTERM    17) SIGCHLD
18) SIGCONT    19) SIGSTOP    20) SIGTSTP    21) SIGTTIN
22) SIGTTOU    23) SIGURG     24) SIGXCPU    25) SIGXFSZ
26) SIGVTALRM  27) SIGPROF    28) SIGWINCH   29) SIGIO
30) SIGPWR
```

Documentation for the software you run on your system often includes
information on the signals that it will respond to. The most important signals you'll need are SIGHUP and SIGKILL. SIGHUP often forces a reload of
configuration information for server processes. However, SIGKILL forces
the command to quit…no matter what. To send one of the signals, use
kill -<signal number> <process ID> <process ID>.

For example, to kill process number 31136

```
>kill -9 31136
[2]+  Killed                 analog /var/log/httpd/access_log
```

If you look at the process listing again, PID 31136 will be gone. It has
been successfully killed.

```
>ps
   PID TTY STAT   TIME COMMAND
18303  p1 R      0:00 ps
30674  p1 S      0:00 /bin/login -h
➥NEW93114217.columbus.here.com -p
30675  p1 S      0:00 -bash
```

Sure enough, kill has done away with process number 31136, and
analog is no longer running on the system.

EXITING A SHELL TO KILL A PROCESS

If you've backgrounded several processes, chances are you don't need to
explicitly kill them when you log out of the system. The shell will send
a SIGHUP signal to all the processes you've started, which will probably

kill them. If you'd like to create a process that will not be killed when you exit your shell, you can do this with nohup.

PREVENTING DEATH: nohup

The nohup command can be prefixed to any other command and will prevent it from being killed with the SIGHUP signal. As you might guess from the name, nohup allows no *HUP*, or *hangup*, signals from killing a process. For example, if I want to prevent my analog process from being killed when I exit the shell, I can run it like this:

```
>nohup analog /var/log/httpd/access_log &
nohup: appending output to `nohup.out'
```

This will run my analog program in the background and prevent it from being killed when I exit my shell. The system also notes that any output that the command produces will be stored in a file called nohup.out.

PROCESS PRIORITY: nice AND renice

Processes that run on Linux have different levels of priority. The amount of priority that a process is given can alter how long it takes to complete, as well as how long other processes on the system might take to run. Processes are given *chunks* of time on the computer's CPU. The level of priority determines how many of these chunks a certain process gets. It isn't wise to run a very computationally intensive task that doesn't need to be finished quickly and have it use up all the processor time on the computer.

Priority levels on Linux range from -20–20, with the default level being 0. Although it might seem a bit backward, -20 is actually the highest priority a process can have, while 20 is the lowest. To control process priority, you use the nice and renice commands.

USING nice

nice is another command that is used as a prefix to the command you want to run. The syntax for nice is **nice -n <priority> <command>**. Continuing the analog example I've been using in this lesson, I'm going to run analog at the lowest level priority I can. Analyzing log files is not a high priority task; there's no sense to run it quickly.

For example

```
>nice -n 20 analog /var/log/httpd/access_log &
```

This puts the `analog` command into the background and assigns it a priority level of `20`. Remember, this is the lowest level priority that a process can have!

 Changing Priorities   Normal users can't set priorities below 0—only the root user can do this. You can think of it as though running the program without `nice` is as high priority as you can get, and you can use the `nice` command to make it nicer for other users.

USING `renice`

Suppose, however, that you've started a command with default priority that has been running for a day, and you have no idea when it's going to finish. This sort of runtime is typical for many scientific and data analysis applications. You figure you might as well lower the priority and let it finish whenever it decides to. You can use `renice` to change the priority of a command that is already running.

To do this, follow these steps:

1. First, you'll need to get a listing of your processes and make a note of the PID that you want to change.

2. Issue the `renice` command using this syntax: **renice *<priority> <process ID>*.**

For example

```
>ps

   PID TTY STAT   TIME COMMAND
  8832  p1 R     0:00 ps
 30674  p1 S     0:00 /bin/login -h
➥NEW93114217.columbus.here.com -p
 30675  p1 S     0:00 -bash
 31136  p1 R     0:00 analog /var/log/httpd/access_log
```

I'm going to change analog (PID 31136) so that it is running with a lower priority. I'll use the `renice` command in this manner:

```
>renice +10 31136

31136: old priority 0, new priority 10
```

PID 31136 is now running with the priority 10, as opposed to the original priority 0.

 Super User Power   It is important to note that only the super user (root) has the capability to raise the priority of a running process. You might only lower the priority of a process—so don't lower a priority thinking you can raise it if it runs too slowly. After it's lowered, it's stuck there unless your system administrator fixes it for you.

CHECKING THE PROCESSES ON YOUR COMPUTER: `top`

Viewing the busy processes on your system is as simple as running the `top` command. `top` displays a continually updating list of processes, the amount of time they are using, as well as the process priority. To exit out of `top`, press the Linux break-sequence (**Ctrl+c**). The processes using the most CPU time are listed at the top of the display.

```
>top

   9:47pm  up 2 days,  5:44,  2 users,  load average:
➥0.07, 0.02, 0.00
83 processes: 82 sleeping, 1 running, 0 zombie, 0 stopped
CPU states:  1.8% user,  4.8% system,  0.0% nice, 93.4% idle
Mem:   63100K av,  57324K used,   5776K free,  34064K shrd,
➥5316K buff
Swap: 128924K av,      0K used, 128924K free
➥36656K cached

   PID USER     PRI  NI  SIZE  RSS SHARE STAT  LIB %CPU %MEM
➥TIME COMMAND
 12448 jray      15   0   740  740   556 R       0  6.5  1.1
```

```
➥0:01 top
12435 root        0    0    692   692    528 S       0   0.1   1.0
➥0:00 in.telnetd
    1 root        0    0    412   412    344 S       0   0.0   0.6
➥0:02 init
    2 root        0    0      0     0      0 SW       0   0.0   0.0
➥0:00 kflushd
    3 root      -12  -12      0     0      0 SW<      0   0.0   0.0
➥0:00 kswapd
  521 root        0    0    888   888    676 S       0   0.0   1.4
➥0:00 CGServer
  498 root        0    0    316   316    260 S       0   0.0   0.5
➥0:00 mingetty
  436 root        0    0    628   628    516 S       0   0.0   0.9
➥0:00 safe_mysqld
  ...
```

There's a ton of information returned, and, if you watch the display, it will update in real-time. You can see the percentage of CPU usage, memory, and lots of other goodies. For more information, view the man page for top.

SCHEDULING COMMANDS: at AND cron

With the capability to run processes in the background comes the capability to schedule processes to run at certain times—even when you're not logged on to the computer. There are two ways to set up your Linux computer to run a command at a certain time. Unfortunately, these might be disabled, depending on the level of control your administrator has chosen to implement. Allowing users to schedule commands for any time they like can be a bit dangerous. The two commands that you'll want to check out are crontab and at.

- **cron**—Runs constantly on your system, and is probably already in use to run log rotation and various cleanup commands on the system. You can create a personal crontab file, which holds information about the interval that you'd like a command to run, and then use the **crontab *<filename>*** command to add your request to the system's crontab file. cron allows you to run commands in intervals as small as a second or as long as a year.

- **at**—Enable you to run a command once, rather than at a repeating interval. This is useful if there is a processor-intensive task that you want to run, and you'd like to run it after business hours so that other tasks aren't affected.

Before you attempt to use either cron or at, you should check with your system administrator. Scheduling processes blindly can affect other users and degrade system performance tremendously if inappropriate processes are scheduled to run simultaneously.

KDE PROCESSES

If you've been playing around in KDE, and I'm sure you have, it's obvious that you can run multiple programs at a single time. Each of these programs runs with its own PID, just as you'd expect. KDE launches each of these programs separately, so they are actually already sharing processor time—no one program is in the foreground or background. You can adjust the process priority from the command line just as you would with any other program. Exiting KDE kills all the active processes you are running.

SUMMARY

You've covered a lot of ground in this lesson. Understanding processes can be a bit difficult at first, but, depending on your use of the system, you might never need to do much more than put a process into the background. If you use KDE exclusively, you'll find that processes work exactly as you would expect on any desktop operating system. Let's review this lesson:

- **&**—The ampersand can be used to put a process into the background. You'll want to use this if you are going to be running something that takes a long time to complete and requires little, if any, user interaction.

- **bg/fg**—The bg and fg commands can be used to move processes to and from background or foreground operation.

- **ps**—To list all the processes that you are running on the system, use the ps command. You can also view processes that are controlled by other users, but you won't be able to modify their priority or kill them (the processes, not the users).

- **kill**—This command is used to send a signal to a process. Normally this signal terminates the execution of the process. In other cases, it can cause a program to re-read its configuration file or reinitialize itself.

- **nohup**—Exiting a shell sends a SIGHUP (hangup) signal to all the running processes in that shell. To enable a process to continue running even after you log off, use the nohup command.

- **nice/renice**—Every process on the computer has a priority. The priority controls how much processor time a process gets in order to complete its task. Priorities range from -20–20, with the negative number being the higher priority.

- **top**—The command top shows the current top CPU-usage processes that are running on the system. The display continuously updates, so you can view how much CPU time new processes take as they are added to the system.

- **at/crontab**—You may schedule commands to run at certain times on your system by using the at and crontab functions. Check with your system administrator and read the appropriate man pages before attempting to do so.

- **KDE**—KDE processes all execute simultaneously. There is no need to worry about backgrounding or foregrounding processes manually. You can, however, adjust the priority of KDE applications from the command line, just as you would with any other process.

LESSON 12
INPUT AND OUTPUT

In this lesson you will learn how to manage Linux process input and output and inter-process communication.

Now that you have learned a bit about working with Linux, its file system, and managing Linux processes, it's time to start putting things together and exploring some of the true power of Linux. In this lesson, you'll also learn about one of the fundamental tools that makes Linux as useful as it is—inter-process communication by input and output redirection.

At the heart of what makes Linux and UNIX so much more powerful than average desktop operating systems is the simple but amazingly effective way in which it abstracts process input and output. To paraphrase the model on which Linux bases input and output, you can imagine that the operating system thinks of user input to a program as a stream—a stream of information. Output from the program back to the user can be thought of in the same fashion. And if the input to the program from the user is a stream of information, why should the operating system care whether a user, a file, or even another program is providing this stream? Once you understand the model of input and output as simply being streams of data, you can immediately see that from the operating system's point of view, the endpoints of these streams are immaterial. So long as the source of the input stream provides the information that the program needs, it does not matter where it comes from. Likewise, provided that the destination of the output stream "behaves like a user," the operating system has no reason to care where the output stream is actually going.

How does Linux make this model available to the user? By providing the concept of input and output *redirection*.

REDIRECTION

To accommodate the user in its streams-of-information–based view of the world, Linux defines certain concepts to which programs must adhere. Specifically, Linux defines several *information connections* for every program, and allows the user to manipulate the source and destination of these connections.

STDIN

The input connection for a program is called *STDIN* (standard input). A program can expect that the incoming data stream from the user (or wherever) will appear at STDIN.

When you interact with a command-line–based program, the program is reading the data you are entering from STDIN. If you prefer not to enter the data by hand, you can put it in a file and *redirect* the file into the program's STDIN.

A program that you can use for an example is `spell`. The `spell` command finds misspellings. Given input on its STDIN, `spell` parses through it, checks the input against a dictionary, and returns any misspellings it finds. Issued from the command line, you can type

```
> spell

   Now is the tyem for all good kiwis to
   come to thie ayde of some very good Linux users
   <Ctrl+d>
```

The **Ctrl+d** finishes the input, and `spell` gets to work, returning the following:

```
tyem
thie
ayde
```

As you might expect, each of the misspelled words is returned. At first glance, this might not appear to be a particularly useful program; however, the `spell` program doesn't care whether it was you typing the input to it, or whether the input came from a file.

Working with spell Actually, it's more proper to think of the spell program as not caring whether the input comes from a file or if a user types it. The spell program was designed to work with input coming from a file or program, it just happens that because of the input/output model, it doesn't mind if the input comes from a user instead. Many programs you'll find on Linux fall into the same category—they are designed to take input or provide output to or from other programs and files. It is only the input/output model that allows direct user interaction with the software, and because of this, you will occasionally find the syntax with which some of these programs converse to be slightly odd. Just remember, they weren't really designed to talk to users.

Use your favorite text editor to create a two-line file containing the same text you typed earlier, and then try spell by redirecting its STDIN. If you named your file reallydumbfile, you can run spell on it by typing

```
> spell < reallydumbfile
```

```
tyem
thie
ayde
```

The < character directs the contents of the file to the right of the character into the STDIN of command to the left.

STDOUT

The *output connection,* which Linux provides for programs, is called *STDOUT* (standard output). Just as you can redirect STDIN from a file, if you want to send the output of a command to a file, you also can redirect STDOUT. The > character directs the STDOUT of the program to the left of the character into the contents of the file to the right of it. For example, if you like looking at the contents of your Web server log file, and you want to put the last 30 lines into a file named kiwis-logs so that you can edit them, you can use the following command:

```
> tail -30 /var/log/httpd/access_log > kiwis-logs
```

This example directs the shell to create the file kiwis-logs and put the STDOUT from the tail command into it. If kiwis-logs already exists, the file is erased before the data is put into it.

If for some reason you collect the end of the log file periodically, you might want to have a complete archive of it. You can direct the shell to append the data to the file, rather than having it clear the file first. To do this, issue the command as

```
> tail -30 /var/log/httpd/access_log >> kiwis-logs
```

The >> character pair appends the STDOUT of the program to the left of the character pair into the file to the right of the character pair.

Of course, you can combine these redirections; if you want to check your spelling and save the results in a file, you can return to your spell command like this:

```
> spell < reallydumbfile > reallydumbspellings
```

STDERR

To make your life easier, Linux actually has two different output streams of data that it defines for programs. The first, STDOUT, you already know about. The second, *STDERR*, is used to allow the program to provide error messages to the user. If the user is redirecting STDOUT and the program can only put errors on STDOUT, the user might never see the errors because they will all go into the redirected file. Instead, programs can use STDERR for errors, and if the user has not redirected it, they can still see error messages and warnings while STDOUT is headed into another file or program.

If you'd like to put STDERR into the same file in which you're storing STDOUT, use &> instead of > in the command.

```
> spell < reallydumbfile &> reallydumbspellings
```

PIPES

Not only can Linux redirect STDIN and STDOUT to and from files, but because these are data streams to Linux, it also provides the idea of *piping* these streams directly between different programs. With pipes you can use the STDOUT of one program directly as the STDIN of another.

To create a pipe in Linux, you use a ¦ character between the programs on the command line.

Again, an example here is so much more illustrative than a lot of words. Take the example of your compulsive collecting of your Web server log files. If instead of collecting them in files, you'd like to amuse and amaze all your friends by sending them the tail end of the file, you can do it without saving it in a file by using the following command:

```
> tail -30 /var/log/httpd/access_log ¦ mail
friend@somewhere.com
```

> **Note**   The mail command is a simple program that lets you send and receive email on your Linux computer. You'll learn more about this and other network utilities in Lesson 18, "Accessing Network Resources."

Thus far, your repertoire of Linux commands probably isn't large enough to make this a truly useful feature, but as you learn more about Linux you will find it is a powerful tool for simplifying your tasks.

For now, one way in which you can make this feature work for you is with piping things into pagers. If you'd like, for example, to be able to page through the output of the ls command, you can pipe it into more. Try typing this:

```
> ls -lRaF ¦ more
```

You will see a particularly long listing of files, which if you don't eventually **Ctrl+c** out of it, will go on for days. Because that's really a complete recursive listing of your entire file system in long format, you're not going to want to use that particular ls command too often. But any time you'd like to page through an ls listing, or any other program output that flows off your screen, you can pipe it into more, (the pager that you learned about in Lesson 7, "Reading Files").

Watch future examples carefully, as the pipe will appear in more useful contexts throughout the rest of this book.

SPLITTING A PIPE: THE tee COMMAND

On occasion, you might have a reason to want to direct STDOUT to a file while continuing to send it down a pipe to another program. In this case, you can use the tee command.

Consider the now-becoming-tedious example of collecting the tail of Web logs. If you aren't satisfied with just emailing it to your friends as in the previous example, you can use the tee command to save it to a file at the same time. You could use

```
> tail -30 /var/log/httpd/access_log ¦ tee kiwis-logs ¦ mail
friend@somewhere.com
```

This helps you out if you want to both save the tail of the file in kiwis-logs and send it to annoy your friend.

SUMMARY

In this lesson, you were introduced to the Linux model of process input and output, and to the easy way in which Linux allows the user to connect programs together to accomplish complex tasks.

- Every program has a STDIN, a STDOUT, and a STDERR. Not all programs use them for user interaction (programs such as Photoshop just don't lend themselves to command-line control), but, for the vast majority that do, these input and output connections can be manipulated.

- You can provide the input data that a program expects on STDIN by hand, from a file, or from another program.

- You can send the STDOUT and STDERR of a program into a file if you'd like to collect it for future use rather than view it as it is produced.

- You can pipe the STDOUT of one program into the STDIN of another.

- One immediately useful thing to do with pipes is to pipe the output of particularly verbose programs into a pager (more, or less).

LESSON 13
REGULAR EXPRESSIONS

In this lesson you will learn the basics behind regular expressions and how to use them with the grep command.

Regular expressions are a wonderful thing. Accept that as a fact as you read through this lesson, and you will be fine. Regular expressions are used in many programming languages and in Linux commands. They are a bit on the esoteric side, but are extremely important to understand nonetheless. Although in this lesson, you'll be looking only at the grep command in conjunction with regular expressions, you can apply this knowledge to most everything that uses regular expressions. Mastering regular expressions will take time. This lesson is rather short and should serve only as an introduction to the topic.

PATTERN MATCHING

Regular expressions are a method of specifying a pattern of characters that can then be matched against existing text. They can be used to locate information when you're not quite sure what you're looking for, or they can perform extremely complex search and replace procedures. The Perl (Practical Extraction and Report Language) programming language uses regular expressions to a great extent, and is considered one of the best languages for creating dynamic Web applications.

SPECIFYING THE REGULAR EXPRESSION IN grep

The format for specifying the regular expression in grep is **grep `<regular expression> <filename> <filename>` ....** Because this lesson uses grep as its example, familiarize yourself with this format. Other programs sometimes require that the regular expression be set off with / on either side of it. This is not the case with grep.

MATCHING SINGLE AND MULTIPLE CHARACTERS: . AND *

Given that a regular expression defines a method of matching, here are some of the most common parts of a regular expression and how they can be used to match a sample pattern. For the examples, I'm going to use a file named sample.txt (if you'd like to follow along, use a text editor from Lesson 8, "Text Editing," to create it now) that looks like this:

```
This is a test
Kim Steinmetz
(614) 555-0591
(615) 555-0000
1998
1999
1800
1750
```

The period character (.) can be used to match any character. For example, let's assume that I don't know how to spell Kim's last name in the preceding file. There's a good chance I could get the *i* and *e* mixed up. In that case, I could use . like this:

```
>grep "St..nmetz" sample.txt

Kim Steinmetz
```

The *St* and *nmetz* make up an obvious part of the regular expression— they match directly with the letters in the name Steinmetz. Because I wasn't sure about the *i* and *e,* I simply replaced them with periods, and grep returned the line I wanted.

The asterisk (*) matches any number of occurrences of a pattern, or portion of a pattern. Suppose I all I knew was that Kim's last name started with an *S* and ended with a *z*. In this case, I could use * in conjunction with . to match anything between an *S* and a *z*:

```
>grep "S.*z" sample.txt

Kim Steinmetz
```

Sure enough, that works well! I guess I can pretty much forget how to spell her name now, huh?

Figuring Out * It is important to note that * will match *any* number of occurrences of a pattern, including zero. This means that the expression s.*z would happily match the string sz. If your expression is turning up matches that you'd hadn't planned on, this might be why.

Use \ to set off a special character. Some characters are used by the shell, so they must be *escaped* using the \ character. You might want to use this in front of characters that *might* be special characters. In most cases it doesn't hurt to use \ if you aren't sure. For example, the shell usually expects you to put double quotes " around strings with spaces in them—it uses the double quote to group the words in the string. If you needed to search through your file for lines containing double quotes, you could not grep for ", instead you would use the following command:

```
> grep \" sample.txt
"special stuff"
```

Using the \ in front of the double quote tells the shell not to attempt to interpret the double quote normally as a surrounding character, but to instead pass it to the grep command for processing.

USING AND NEGATING RANGES IN A REGULAR EXPRESSION: [ ] AND ^

You might have noticed that the sample.txt file I've been using has a few dates inside. Suppose I only want to match the years that fall in the 1700–1800s. To do this, I can use a range, which is specified in a regular expression as **[<starting point>-<ending point>]** The starting and ending points can be numbers or ranges within the alphabet.

For example

```
>grep "1[7-8][0-9]*" sample.txt
1800
1750
```

My pattern states that any valid matches must start with a 1 and be followed by a number in the range of 7–8, followed by one or several numbers in the range of 0–9. Ranges can help you pull certain values out of files. You can expand the capability of the range by applying the negation operator.

The caret (^) negates a range if it is used at the start of the range specification. Negating a range matches the opposite of what the range matches.

For example

```
>grep "1[^7-8][0-9]*" sample.txt

(614) 555-0591
(615) 555-0000
1998
1999
```

Notice that I now match anything that isn't in the 1700 or 1800s. I also match two phone numbers that, if you look at the last two digits of the area codes, do indeed match the pattern I've specified.

MATCHING THE START AND END OF A LINE: ^ (AGAIN) AND $

In order to uniquely match the years in the sample file, I can use the start-of-line and end-of-line regular expression characters to stop grep from matching the phone numbers. These characters are commonly called *anchors* because they anchor a pattern to the start or end of a line. Since 1998 and 1999 are both at the beginning of a line, this should be easy.

- ^—Used outside of a range, the ^ character matches the start of a line.

- $—This matches the end of a line. If your pattern falls at the end of a line, you can anchor it in this position with $.

For example

```
>grep "^1[^7-8][0-9]*" sample.txt

1998
1999
```

That's more like it. Only the two dates are returned, because they fall at the beginning of a line. The phone numbers no longer match because the portion that did match is not at the start of the line.

USES FOR REGULAR EXPRESSIONS

What you've just learned is only a very tiny subset of the regular expressions that you can generate. Regular expressions can be used in a wide variety of different applications. For example, sed, the stream editor, can replace patterns of text from a stream of text on-the-fly. Being able to do a global regular expression search and replace on a thousand files rather than editing each one individually is wonderful. When you are using the shell you can also use a subset of the complete regular expression library to specify filenames for operations.

For example, if you have a group of files named test1, test2, test3, test4, and test5, and you'd like to copy files 3 through 5 to a new directory, you could use a regular expression like this:

```
>cp test[3-5] newdirectory
```

You'll need to consult the man pages for the shell you are running in order to determine the regular expressions that it supports. The same goes for everything else that uses regular expressions. Unfortunately, even though regular expressions themselves are pretty standard, the extent to which an individual application supports them is entirely up to that application. Perl, for example, is an application (and, in turn, is a complete programming environment) that makes extensive use of regular expressions.

With the growing popularity of the World Wide Web comes the need to process user-supplied information quickly and reliably. Unfortunately, there is little control over what sort of information a user might submit on a form or other interactive Web document. If you intend to do Web programming, you will find that regular expressions are a lifesaver and can be used to extract data from a form and turn it into a usable format. If this sounds interesting to you, I strongly suggest looking into the Perl programming language.

SUMMARY

Regular expressions are an extremely flexible way of describing a pattern to be matched. Because many Linux applications, including the shell, support regular expressions, it is important to develop a general understanding of how they work and what they are good for. Let's review:

- .—This matches any character. Use it whenever you aren't sure what character will fall in a specific position.

- *—Using the * will match any number of occurrences of a specific pattern. You can use this in conjunction with . or ranges.

- \—Special characters need to be escaped using the \ character. If you need to use the quote character (") in a pattern, for example, you'll have to escape it.

- **Ranges**—You can match ranges of numbers or letters to limit a pattern. Ranges are enclosed in brackets ([ ]). To negate a range, use ^ at the start of the range specification.

- ^/$—These two special characters match the start and end of a line, respectively. They are commonly referred to as anchors because they anchor a pattern to a specific place on a line.

- **Regular expressions**—These are used in many Linux programs and can be an extremely powerful tool. Read the man pages for your shell and other utilities in order to determine the extent to which they support regular expressions.

LESSON 14
BASIC SHELL SCRIPTING

In this lesson, you will learn a bit more of the magic behind automation and customization using shell scripts.

In Lesson 12, "Input and Output," you learned about pipes, and you probably began to see a bit of what makes Linux so powerful and configurable. What you probably didn't realize is that using a pipe is only the very beginning of what Linux can do to customize and automate tasks. As you read through this lesson, you'll see that pipes are only the smallest tip of the iceberg.

Shell scripts are essentially programs written in the language of the shell. If you're a user from the pre-Windows days of the PC, you'll recognize shell scripts as being similar to BATCH files. Macintosh users, while not burdened with a command line in day-to-day life, should still see the similarity to the AppleScript and Frontier scripting languages. While anything larger than a few dozen lines of script would probably be better done in a language other than the shell, thinking of shell scripts as *little* programs does injustice to the flexibility and convenience that they provide the user.

GETTING A LOT FOR A LITTLE: SHELL SCRIPTS

You would usually create a shell script when you want to combine a set of actions that you routinely need to repeat into a single convenient action.

For example, if you're in the habit of coming in to work, sending all your coworkers an email message saying "Howdy Neighbor," firing off a print job to print out the most recent 100 hits to your personal Web page, and then opening an *xterm* and reading a few newsgroups, you can save yourself some time and keystrokes by writing a little shell script to do all this automatically. You could put it all in a file and name it something such as `save-timesave-time`, and in the future, you'd just have to come in to work and type **save-timesave-time** to automatically save yourself some time!

Another instance of using shell scripts, or shell scripting techniques, is with some commands that can be used to automate certain tasks directly in the shell, without having to be put in a file. You will look primarily at these, because they're easier to learn and more immediately useful. As you get more comfortable with Linux you'll naturally gravitate to the idea of just putting what you're typing in a file, and another shell script programmer will be born.

SHELL SCRIPT FILES

As mentioned earlier, shell scripts are small programs written in the same language that you use to talk to the shell. It only makes sense that you can do this with Linux—remember the Linux model of input and output? The shell really doesn't care whether it's you issuing commands to it, or if the commands are coming to it from some other source, such as a file.

As a quick introduction to the sort of thing you can do with a shell script file, take the `save-timesave-time` example. If you wanted to actually write a shell script to do exactly this, you need to put together a few of the tools you've seen so far, and a few more that you haven't yet. However, for your edification, here's what to do:

1. Determine the name of your Web server log; here, /var/log/httpd/access_log is assumed.

2. Determine your username. (You'd better know this one by now!) For the purposes of this example, you're named Bob, and your email address is bob@very.important.com.

3. Figure out how to send email to a bunch of people with one command. This sort of behavior is generally frowned upon unless it's for good reason, so you'll just send yourself email here.

4. Figure out how you read news. Here, the `trn` command is used.

5. Learn where the binary for your shell is. If you're using csh, csh. /bin/csh is assumed here. If you're not using csh, you should be for the purpose of writing shell scripts that are compatible with other Linux and UNIX machines. To switch temporarily to csh, type **csh** at a command prompt.

6. Figure out how to print on your system.

7. Create the shell script file vi save-time.

8. Add the following lines to the shell script file:

```
#!/bin/csh
echo "Howdy Neighbor" ¦ mail bob@very.important.com
grep "bob" /usr/local/httpd/logs/access_log ¦ tail -1100
➥¦ lpr
xterm -e trn &
exit
```

9. Save the file and exit your editor. In vi, **:wq!<Return>**.

10. Change the file attributes on the file so that you can execute it: **chmod 755 save-time**.

11. Execute your new shell script: **./save-time**.

 Tip   You might be able to type **save-time** if the current directory is in your PATH environment variable (echo $PATH to check).

Your script should, if everything worked, produce exactly the results that were outlined at the beginning of this section.

To explain a few of the things that happened in this shell script the following might be helpful—most of this should be understandable from what you've learned thus far:

- The echo command puts things on its STDOUT. Here, it is used to create a STDOUT stream containing "Howdy Neighbor," which is then fed to mail's STDIN via a pipe.

- The `mail` command can take a message on STDIN and send it to
  a list of recipients—more on `mail` in Lesson 18, "Accessing
  Network Resources."

- You know what `grep` does, and what `tail` does. After the last
  100 lines matching *bob* have been found, they're handed to `lpr`
  on its STDIN. `lpr` sends data to a printer—more on `lpr` in
  Lesson 17, "Printing."

- `xterm`, which starts a terminal, can be told to start a program
  running in the terminal window by using the `-e` option.

So Many Shells on the Beach

As has probably become apparent to you if you've spent as much time
playing with your Linux account as you have reading this book, Linux has
an abundance of shells available for you to use. The syntax and available
commands in each of these shells ranges from subtly to extremely different. For the purposes of this lesson, you'll be using commands and syntax
compatible with `csh` and `tcsh`.

The Bourne shell, `sh`, is probably the best shell to write scripts in if you're
concerned about distributing large sophisticated scripts to unknown users.
It's not the easiest shell to use at the command line though, so you're better off starting with the same shell you use in day-to-day life.

Doing It Again and Again: `foreach`

Instead of spending time looking at collecting commands into a file to
automate them, you can get a lot of mileage out of simple automation
techniques that don't involve putting commands in files at all. One of the
commands used for this is the `foreach` command.

Executing a Command Over and Over

If you find yourself in a situation where you need to repeatedly execute
some action for each set of files, the `foreach` command can help. It takes
a list of files and does something *for each* of them. The use is much easier
to demonstrate than to explain. If you have a list of files you need to do
something to, you can do the following to use `foreach`:

1. Figure out what *something* you want to do. In this example, you've got a bunch of directories, and you want to create a tar file of each.

2. Figure out the names of the files/directories that you want to do your something to. In this case, you're going create tar files for the directories mydirectory, yourdirectory, and herdirectory.

3. Pick a variable; here you're just going to use a variable named test. It doesn't matter what the variable name is, just so long as it doesn't conflict with the name of the command.

4. Issue the foreach command as **foreach** *<variablename>* *(<filenames>)*. The foreach command will then ask you what you want to do for each file by displaying a question mark. Fill this in with whatever you need to do. Again, you're going to be tarring files in this example. After giving the command for whatever it is you want to do, finish it by putting the command end on a line by itself.

To illustrate the example, if you really wanted to do this, you would type

```
> foreach test (mydirectory yourdirectory herdirectory)
? tar -cvf $test.tar $test
? end
```

Your machine will respond by defining the variable test, and then running the tar command for each file you gave it to work with. Inside the foreach command loop, you will note the use of the expression $test. foreach goes through the list of filenames you gave it, and puts each one sequentially in the test variable. To use the contents of a variable in the shell, put a $ sign before it. For example, foreach first puts mydirectory in the variable test. It then runs the tar command, and the shell expands the test variable to mydirectory. The tar command that gets executed actually looks like this: tar -cvf mydirectory.tar mydirectory. The next time the loop foreach puts yourdirectory in the variable test, and the process is repeated.

You can use regular expressions in the shell instead of enumerating the filenames to use the foreach command. If you notice in the previous example, all the directories you want to tar actually have part of their names in common—*directory* in this instance. If you want to produce the same results without having to enumerate all the directory names to foreach, you could issue the foreach command as **foreach test (*directory)**. You can use the pattern matching tools you learned about in Lesson 13, "Regular Expressions," to match any collection of filenames you want.

RENAMING MULTIPLE FILES

You've probably noticed that the mv command can't do some things that would be really convenient, such as renaming multiple files with new names instead of new locations—an ideal problem for foreach.

For example, imagine you have a bunch of files for a pet project, and they're named things such as brokenjunk.start, brokenjunk.today, brokenjunk.gif, and so on. All the sudden your boss decides that it's important and that you have to give these files to the development department because they want to demo your project next week. This never happens to you, right? If it did, you might want to rename your files to something a little more professional. Instead of renaming the files one by one, you can use the foreach command to automate the task for you. In this case you might type

```
> foreach test (brokenjunk.*)
? mv $test importantstuff.$test:e
? end
```

The part of this you might not immediately understand is the $test:e part. This says "expand the $test variable, and toss out everything except for the stuff after the last . in the filename"—in this case, the parts that make the files different (start, today, and so on).

Of course, this isn't a very useful command for three files, but if you've got a project with hundreds of files, it could save you a lot of typing.

MODIFYING AND REPLACING ORIGINALS

Another useful trick that you can use the foreach command for is when you need to apply a process to each of the many files, and you want to do it without creating new files.

Let's say you have a collection of image files, each of which have a border that you want to crop off, and then you want to scale them to a smaller size. If the imaginary command crop took files on STDIN and wrote its data to STDOUT, you could use the foreach command similar to this:

```
> foreach test (*.gif)

? crop < $test > holding
? mv holding $test
? end
```

Why not just do crop < $test > $test? Because you can't be guaranteed that you can get away with writing to the file while you're still reading from it—so you store the results in a temporary file named *holding*. Follow up by using the mv command to move the temporary file back to the original filename.

DOING IT AFTER A WHILE: sleep

The utility of a command that just sits there for a while is perhaps not readily apparent, but you'll use it in the next example. If you do run across a situation where you need a shell script to pause for a while, you can use the sleep command. Issue the sleep command as **sleep <seconds>**, and the shell will halt until that many seconds have passed; then it will resume execution of whatever it was doing.

DOING IT CONDITIONALLY: while AND if

If you'd like to get sophisticated with the control of your automation, you can turn to conditional statements that can activate certain sections of your script only when certain conditions apply.

To use conditional statements, you need to create a condition for the statement to test. This can be as complicated as you like, but for now, you should stick to simple things such as equal to.

USING while

The while command, with the syntax while *(<condition>)* does things *while* a certain condition holds.

Consider the situation where you're feeling really lonely and want to get some email. When you execute /bin/mail, all it tells you is No mail. A sad day indeed. So, to try to brighten your day, you've written yourself a little script that sends email to a few of your friends every so often, asking them to email you back. Of course you don't want to be such a bozo that it keeps sending them email even after they've replied, so you want it to stop after you've received email, or only continue while you don't receive email.

If you actually wanted to try this, you could do so by entering a script such as the following:

```
> set hopeful=(`/bin/mail ¦ grep -cv No`)

> while ($hopeful==0)

? echo "please send me mail" ¦ mail myfriend@somewhere.com
? echo "please send me mail" ¦ mail
↪anotherfriend@elsewhere.com
? sleep 60
? set hopeful=(`/bin/mail ¦ grep -cv No`)
? end
```

This silly little script is making use of grep to count the lines (-c option) that *do not* (-v option) contain a match for No, and assigning the result to the variable named hopeful. Putting the /bin/mail piped into the grep command inside single back quotes causes the shell to execute those commands and return their output, which is what gets assigned to the variable hopeful.

Because you don't have mail, and the only response that mail gives when you don't is No mail, there are zero lines that don't contain No initially.

The script uses mail to send out a few pathetic pleas, and then goes to *sleep* for 60 seconds. Afterward, it checks the status of your mailbox again. If you've received mail in the interim, mail will give headers instead of the No mail response. In this case, there should be a number other than zero lines which don't match No. (Of course, presuming you're not such an unlucky person that your friends reply "No, we won't reply; go away!") If there are lines that don't contain No, hopeful won't be equal to zero, and the while will terminate. If hopeful is still zero, well, your friends' mailboxes will fill up pretty fast.

USING if

The if command works in much the same way as the while command, only it doesn't loop; it simply executes one command based on the condition. The syntax of the if command is **if (*<condition>*) *<command>*.**

Using another silly example, if you're irritated by the fact that you have no email, and just hate seeing that No mail response, you can use a shell script to do something about it. You could try creating yourself a shell script file named checkmail with the following contents:

```
#!/bin/csh
set foo=(`/bin/mail ¦ grep -cv No`)
if ($foo == 0) echo "You poor guy"
```

Again, it's going to use /bin/mail to find out whether you have mail, and if you don't have mail, your computer will commiserate with you.

SUMMARY

Shell scripting can allow you to add functionality and customize your environment. You have the option of doing things as sophisticated as creating small programs, or as simple as automating your daily repetitive tasks. Let's review the key points of this lesson:

- Your shell scripts can be stored in files to allow you to execute many commands by simply typing one.

- There are many different shells—yours might work differently than what is presented here, but probably has similar capabilities. If it doesn't, get a better shell! What you've learned in this lesson applies to csh, which is a very commonly used shell for programming scripts.

- The foreach command allows you to repeat a set of commands for each of a number of files

- The `while` command allows you to repeat a set of commands while a certain condition holds.

- The `if` command allows you to execute a command or not execute it, based on a conditional statement.

- The `sleep` command does nothing for a while—sometimes this is actually useful.

LESSON 15
USER UTILITIES

In this lesson, you will learn how to change your password, shell, and other information.

Linux provides a wealth of utilities that help you control the information that the system stores for your user account. In this lesson, you'll see how to monitor the use of your system through some useful command-line utilities.

CHANGING YOUR PASSWORD: `passwd` AND `yppasswd`

One of the most important things you'll need to do in a networked environment is change your password. Passwords should generally be changed on a somewhat frequent basis in order to maintain a secure environment. There are two ways that a password can be changed. If you are in a networked environment you might have to use the yppasswd which will update your password on all of the networked machines. The most obvious way of telling if this is the sort of environment you're working in is if you can log in to multiple computers with the same username and password and access the same information. This is a common setup for Linux/UNIX computer labs. If your machine is an isolated Linux computer, just use the passwd command and you should be fine. Both operate in an identical manner; it is where the updated password is stored that is different.

For example

```
>passwd

Changing password for jray
Old password: *****
New password: ******
Retype new Linux password: ******
passwd: all authentication tokens updated successfully
```

The passwords you type are not echoed to the display as you type them. I've included a few asterisks to show that typing is taking place. If the password change is successful, Linux will indicate that with the All authentication tokens updated successfully message. Linux, in some cases, will keep you from choosing certain passwords if they are too short, or based on words in its built-in dictionary file. You should choose passwords that are not based on common words and that mix letters, numbers, and letter cases.

CHANGING YOUR SHELL: chsh

In the beginning of this book, you learned that there are a variety of different shells that you can run. Now you're going to learn how to change them. The chsh command lets you choose one of the shells that is registered for use on the machine. Before you actually change the shell, you might want to see the shells that are available on your computer. Do this with the chsh -1 command.

```
>chsh -1

/bin/bash
/bin/sh
/bin/ash
/bin/bsh
/bin/tcsh
/bin/csh
/bin/ksh
```

There are currently seven different shells that I can choose from. I'm going to go ahead and change to ksh from my current choice, bash.

For example

```
>chsh

Changing shell for jray.
Password: *****
New shell [/bin/bash]: /bin/ksh
Shell changed.
```

The next time I log in to Linux, I'll be in ksh instead of bash. You probably won't ever need to change your shell, unless the default shell on your system is the Bourne shell (sh). If you'd like to try other shells, feel free. You can always change back.

GETTING AND CHANGING USER INFORMATION: finger AND chfn

Each user has a few pieces of information about his or her location stored as part of the system password file. This enables other users to quickly find the information necessary to contact them. The command that displays this user data is finger. Because the user information is stored when the user account is created, chances are you don't have any information set for your account. In order to change that, you'll use chfn.

USING finger

Using the finger command is simple. Just use finger <username> to get information about a user who is local to your system. To get information about someone on a remote system, you can try finger <username>@<remote host>. Depending on how the remote host is configured and the type of remote host, it might or might not work.

For example

```
>finger jray@poisontooth.com

[poisontooth.com]
Login: jray                          Name: John Ray
Directory: /home/jray                Shell: /bin/bash
On since Sun Nov 29 16:35 (EST) on ttyp0 from 192.168.0.91
    6 hours 47 minutes idle
No mail.
No Plan.
```

There isn't much of interest that is returned here. This is because I haven't set any personal information yet. You can see, however, how long I've been logged in to the system, as well as my real name and my home directory. I can add personal information to my account profile with chfn.

USING chfn

The chfn command runs an interactive process that enables you to set some personal information for your account. Run chfn on a command line without any options.

```
>chfn
```

```
Changing finger information for jray.
Password: *****
Name [John Ray]: John Ray
Office []: 7879 Rhapsody Drive
Office Phone []: (614) XXX-XXXX
Home Phone []: (614) XXX-XXXX
```

I can change or set my full name, my office address, and home and office phone numbers. If you'd rather not set a value, don't—you aren't forced to supply any of this information, unless it is the policy of your company. Now that I've added some information about myself, I'll re-run the finger command to see the results.

```
>finger jray@poisontooth.com
```

```
[poisontooth.com]
Login: jray                          Name: John Ray
Directory: /home/jray                Shell: /bin/bash
Office: 7879 Rhapsody Drive
➥Office Phone: (614) XXX-XXXX
Home Phone: (614) XXX-XXXX
On since Sun Nov 29 16:35 (EST) on ttyp0 from 192.168.0.91
    6 hours 48 minutes idle
On since Sun Nov 29 21:47 (EST) on ttyp1 from 192.168.0.211
No mail.
No Plan.
```

That's a bit better! Now my office address and office and home phone numbers are shown. Depending on how you use your system, you might not want to set any of this information. If that's the case, feel free to wipe the chfn command from your memory.

MONITORING YOUR SYSTEM: date, uptime, AND who

Now turn your attention to a few commands that you can use to monitor your system. It's nice to be able to see who is logged in to your machine as well as the current status of the computer. Here is a quick look at a trio of commands that will show you information that you might find useful to check on your computer.

USING date

The date command, as you might have guessed, returns the current date and time. If you have Super User privileges you can also use date to set the day and time on the computer. Ordinary user accounts do not have this capability.

```
>date
```

```
Mon Nov 30 01:15:17 EST 1998
```

There's nothing to it. You might be wondering why I would even take the space to cover such a command. The answer is simple: Without the date command, how do you find out the current day and time information on your computer? KDE displays the information on its desktop, but outside of KDE, the date command will become very useful when you have stared at your screen for several hours on end and lost all sense of time.

USING uptime

uptime is another simple and useful command. It returns the current time, the number of users logged in to the system, how long the system has been running, and the amount of load that the system has been under. Just type uptime at the command prompt.

```
>uptime
```

```
1:20am  up 2 days,  9:18,  2 users,  load average:
➥1.10, 0.90, 0.10
```

As you can see from this result, its 1:20 a.m. (yes, it really is!); my system has been running for 2 days, 9 hours, and 18 minutes since it was last rebooted. There are currently two users logged in to the system. The load average is comprised of three values: The first value is the load on the system over the past minute, the second is the average load over 10 minutes, and the third, over 15 minutes. These values are rarely higher than 1 or 2. If you see a system load average of anything over 5, your computer is *really* busy.

USING who

As you know, Linux is a multi-user system. This means that there can be several different users logged in at a time. If your system seems slow, you might want to check who is using the computer so you can run over to their desk and yell at them. To see who is logged on, you use the who command.

```
>who

jray      ttyp0      Nov 29 16:35 (192.168.0.91)
yort      ttyp1      Nov 29 21:47 (192.168.0.211)
```

There are currently two users logged in to the system. who returns the username of each user logged in, as well as the name of the controlling terminal, the date and time they logged in, and the IP address they are connected from.

Tip   If you don't recognize one of the users connected to your system, remember the `finger` command. You can use it to find out more information about other users on the system.

OTHER COMMAND LINE AND KDE UTILITIES

There are hundreds of other utilities available on your system for monitoring network connections, processing files, and even generating calendars (`cal`). If you'd like to explore, I suggest listing the files in the /usr/bin and /usr/local/bin directories and reading the man pages for anything that sounds interesting.

The KDE environment provides its own utilities including a PIM (Personal Information Manager) called KArm, a floppy formatter called KFloppy, and a CD player called KCD, and so on. There is simply no way a single reference book can touch on all these topics completely. Your best bet is to look through the file system and research the commands that look interesting. The extensive man page collection available for command-line utilities provides excellent reference information. KDE also provides comprehensive online help, which should make life pretty easy.

SUMMARY

Linux has tons of built-in utilities. In this lesson, you learned about several of the programs that modify information related to your account profile, as well as a few utilities to monitor the state of your computer and who is currently using it. Take a look at what else is discussed in this lesson:

- **passwd/yppasswd**—The passwd command changes your account password. If you're in an environment with networked Linux computers, you may have to use the yppasswd command instead.

- **chsh**—Use the change shell command to change your current shell. If you don't know for sure which shell you want to switch to, you can use chsh -l to list the available shells on your system.

- **finger**—This command looks up personal information about an account on your computer or on a remote computer. finger is sometimes disabled for security reasons, so you may not be able to use finger to get the results you expect.

- **chfn**—Change finger information using this command. This lets you change your full name, as well as the office address and office/home phone numbers in your account profile.

- **date**—Simple enough, date displays the current day and time on your computer.

- **uptime**—The uptime command provides a summary of information about the state of your operating system, including the length of time it has been online, the number of users logged on, and the average load on your system for the past 15 minutes.

- **who**—who lets you see all the users who are logged in to your computer, the date that they connected, and what network address they are connected from. If your machine seems slow, you might want to use who to find out where all the processor time is going.

- **Other utilities**—There are far too many utilities on the system to cover them all in this book. Luckily, the man pages provide extensive documentation for most programs on the system. In addition, KDE has its own comprehensive documentation system.

LESSON 16

MODIFYING THE USER ENVIRONMENT

In this lesson, you'll learn about the tools you need to modify your environment and the way that some commands work for you.

There are a vast number of programs that all work together to create the Linux user experience; it's because of this that you'll need to learn to use the tools from this lesson in conjunction with the documentation for your programs to make the modifications you desire.

 Shell Assumption This lesson is going to assume that you're using bash as your shell. If you are using a different shell, some of the syntax will need to be changed, but the ideas remain the same.

ALIASES

One of the most useful features that shells provide to the user is the ability to create command aliases. Aliases are, quite simply, aliases. If, for example, you're a long-time DOS user, you might find yourself typing **del** instead of **rm** to delete files. Want to change this? Set an alias with the alias command. The syntax is **alias <newname> <command to run>**. If you'd actually like to make that alias for del, you would type **alias del rm**. After setting this alias, any time you type **del**, it will execute the rm command.

More useful than simply renaming commands, you can use the alias command to create meta commands that enforce certain options. For example, it's always a good idea to force rm to be in Interactive mode (rm -i). To do this with an alias, you can type **alias rm 'rm -i'** (note the direction of the single quotes). Now whenever you type rm, it will actually execute rm -i instead.

If you'd like to get really sophisticated with aliases, you can even build little multi-command scripts inside aliases. For example, consider the situation where you want to access two different news servers from your account. In this case, perhaps it's a public server for regular Usenet newsgroups, and a corporate server for internal news. The trn and rn commands only understand one news server at a time, and worse, save the "what I have read" information in a file with a fixed name. What to do? Use the alias command to automate things for you. The following two aliases will solve your problem.

```
> alias readcorporate 'export NNTPSERVER=
➡server.big.company.com;\
                      cp ~/.corp-newsrc ~/.newsrc;\
                      trn;
                      cp ~/.newsrc ~/.corp-newsrc'
> alias readpublic    'export NNTPSERVER=
➡public.newsstand.com;\
                      cp ~/.public-newsrc ~/.newsrc;\
                      trn;
                      cp ~/.newsrc ~/.public-newsrc'
```

What do they do?

- The first line of each sets an environment variable which tells trn where to look to get its news. More on this in the next section.

- The second line of each copies a setting file to the file .newsrc in your home directory. The trn command uses the file .newsrc to keep track of what news you've read and what is new news. If you're using two different servers with two different sets of newsgroups, you unfortunately can't use the same .newsrc file, so you'll need to keep two of them around and let the alias copy the correct one for you when you need it.

- The third line should be self-explanatory. The trn command reads Usenet newsgroups. A little more on this in Lesson 18, "Accessing Network Resources."

- The fourth line might be a bit of a mystery at first, but it's really quite simple as well. Because the trn command will update the .newsrc file with information on what you've just read, you want to preserve the file for the next time you read news, so you copy it back to its holding location.

Now all you have to do is type **readcorporate** to read your news from your corporate news server server.big.company.com. And to read your public Usenet newsgroups you type **readpublic**.

ENVIRONMENT VARIABLES

As mentioned earlier in this book, most of the software you use, and the interface you work in when using Linux, is configured with seemingly cryptic text files. Other pieces of software are configured by special shell variables called *environment variables*. (You should remember shell variables from Lesson 14, "Basic Shell Scripting.")

Environment variables are used by programs to pick up specific pieces of information that are needed to run. For example, you might run across programs that want an environment variable that contains the path to their Help file information. Others use environment variables to contain custom settings for things such as window size or placement preferences. In the preceding aliases section, you might have noticed a program that wanted an environment variable set to tell it what Internet host to contact.

Environment variables aren't set using quite the same syntax as regular shell variables, so instead of using **set** *<variablename>=<value>*, you would use the syntax **export** *<variablename>=<value>*.

Consider the situation where you have a program that says to set the environment variable HELPFILE_LOC to the directory containing its help information. Unless this variable is set, it can't find the information it needs, and it won't work properly. If you've found that the Help file is located in the directory /usr/local/helpstuff, you can set the variable you need by using this command: **export HELPFILE_LOC=/usr/local/helpstuff**.

The number of programs that use environment variables for configuration information is quite large, but the format is always the same. All you need to do is find out what variable needs to be set, and then set it to the correct value.

 Seeing Shell Variables   If you'd like to see the environment variables that are already set in your shell, you can use the `export` command with no arguments.

If you're running X Windows and trying to display on a different machine than you're running the client, you might have to set the DISPLAY variable: **export DISPLAY=<machinename>:0.0**.

If you've run a program and it exits with a complaint such as `ld.so not found`, you might have to set the LD_LIBRARY_PATH with a command such as **export LD_LIBRARY_PATH=/usr/local/lib**.

The possibilities really are endless—thankfully, making the settings is a relatively painless process. Just remember that the settings you make in one shell do not affect other shells. You can have the same environment variable set to different values in different shells you're running simultaneously if you need to access more than one configuration at a time.

PATHS

Another special shell variable is the PATH variable. It tells the shell where to look for programs to execute for you. Remember how long the `find` command took to find things for you in Lesson 5, "Finding Files"? You wouldn't want it to take that long every time you try to execute a program, so you don't want the system to have to search through everything on your machine to find a program. Instead, the shell keeps a short list of where to look for programs, and it only searches these locations.

You might notice that if you have a copy of a program in your current directory, in some cases typing the filename will result in a `command not found` error. This is because it's common for the PATH variable to lack the current directory. You can either execute programs in the current directory by typing **./<programname>**, or by adding the current directory to your path.

Working with Paths   The current directory is usually left out of the path because including it is a bit of a security risk. If the current directory is in your path, you can potentially be fooled into executing arbitrary programs by naming them as common Linux commands and sneaking them into your directories. If you want to put the current directory in your path, always put it at the end of the path. That way normal Linux commands will be found before any Trojan horses that may have made their way into your system.

If you'd like to see what your current path is, you can do so by using echo $PATH. If it's missing some paths you need, say the current directory and /usr/local/bin, you can add these by using the command **export PATH=$PATH:.:/usr/local/bin**.

USERS DEFAULTS: THE DOT FILES

Your account configures certain features for you automatically when you log in and when you start shells. Programs other than the shell also occasionally use *dot files* to hold configuration information. Dot files are, literally, files with names starting with the . character, and you're likely to find an abundance already populating your home directory. Some common files are

- **.login and .logout**—As you might guess, files which are executed when you log in and when you log out, respectively. If you look in these files you will find that they are shell scripts which use commands that you are already familiar with. The login shell script is typically used for things such as swapping in various sets of configuration files if you want to set up multiple different environments for yourself, and for doing other things that need to be handled automatically at login. The logout script is used much less frequently, but it can contain useful things you need to do at logout time. What sort of use could you make of the .login and .logout files? How about adding commands that echo the date and time information into a file whenever you log in and log out. If you've ever had to fill out a timesheet, you'll find this one appealing.

- **.bashrc** or **.bash_profile**—Shell scripts that are executed when you open bash. (Other shells will have their own scripts that execute at startup as well. Check with your shell's documentation on this.) Again, you should be familiar with the syntax. In this file, you can put in commands that do things such as add custom paths to your environment, set environment variables, and set up any aliases you might be interested in.

- **.plan**—A file that contains information that your system will send back to anyone who fingers you. Users typically use their .plan file to contain contact information, favorite quotes, and anecdotes. Put things in your plan that you would want people to see when they try to look you up from remote.

- **.Xdefaults**—This file contains settings that are used by the server resource database. The syntax of this file is covered briefly in Lesson 3, "The Graphical User Interface." In general you won't need to modify this file, but you can configure many options regarding how the X server treats various programs and how various X11 programs work here. If you choose to poke around in it, be sure to make a backup copy of it first, in case you have to put it back. After you have made a backup though, don't be afraid to make modifications. The syntax is straightforward, and if you've survived this far, you can probably figure out how to make most of the modifications you might want to try.

You'll undoubtedly find that you have other dot files in your directories as well. Don't be afraid to look in them. You'll find most to be more readable than you might think. While it might be a bit intimidating at first, a large part of making Linux work for you is customizing your environment by modifying these files. Make backups first, but don't be afraid to experiment—it's half the joy of using Linux!

FIXING BROKEN TERMINALS: stty

On occasion, you might find yourself in a command-line window that seems to have gone slightly nuts. The Delete key produces ^?, the Backspace key makes a ^H, and Ctrl+c shows ^C. If this happens to you, you need to reset the terminal parameters for erase and interrupt. To do this, enter the two following commands:

```
> stty erase <delete>
> stty intr ^c
```

Note that in place of typing a control character directly, you can use ^<character> to represent the character. You can also use stty erase Backspace if your keyboard layout makes Backspace more convenient than Delete. If your terminal has gone completely insane and the Return key no longer seems to be working correctly, you can try using the command: stty sane Ctrl+j. This command will attempt to reset the terminal to its default settings, but isn't guaranteed to work.

CHANGING KDE'S APPEARANCE

KDE includes the capability to customize your desktop environment just as you would under Windows or Mac OS. You can set the background, screensaver, fonts, and other attributes of the windowing environment. The changes you make affect only your personal settings (they are not system wide), so feel free to customize to your heart's content! A sampling of the different settings that you can use to customize your desktop are shown in Figure 16.1.

To change KDE's appearance:

1. Click the main K toolbar menu item.

2. Choose Settings from the menu.

3. Select the property you want to change (Desktop, Sound, and so forth).

4. Choose any appropriate sub-property from the category you've chosen. (For example, choosing Desktop allows you to change colors, background, and fonts among others.)

5. Make the changes you'd like, and then click the **Apply** or **OK** to set them.

6. Enjoy!

FIGURE 16.1   KDE offers a wide selection of custom configuration options.

SUMMARY

In this lesson, you were introduced to the idea of modifying your environment settings by the use of aliases, environment variables, and configuration files. Making these modifications is what lets you make the environment you work in your own. Let's review what is covered in this lesson:

- **Environment variables**—Frequently used for specifying single configuration options to a program, such as providing a pointer to a directory that the program needs.

- **PATH variable**—Keeps track of where the system searches for commands when you type them. If a command exists on the system, but the path to the command is not in your PATH variable, it will not be found when you type the command name.

- **Aliases**—A powerful feature of Linux shells. They allow you to rename commands, or cause commands to always use certain options when you issue them.

- **Dot files**—Many programs use text files containing configuration information for control purposes. These files almost universally have filenames that start with a . character. They are the place to look for automating settings to your shell and configuring options for the windowing system.

- **stty**—A command that can rescue your terminal session if something has caused it to begin behaving oddly.

Don't be afraid to experiment. You've just made it through a lesson on modifying your user environment. Now go out and do it!

LESSON 17
PRINTING

In this lesson you'll learn how you can print requests (jobs) to a printer on your network.

Setting up a printer varies from printer to printer and requires Super User (root) privileges, so it is difficult to demonstrate this task in the book. Linux computers often speak to lpd servers that provide access to remote printers across a TCP/IP network. Luckily, both local printers (directly-connected) and remote printers are accessed in the same fashion, so it is possible to show you how you can use a printer in a generic fashion that will apply no matter how your system administrator has configured your computer.

SENDING A PRINT JOB: lpr

In Linux, multiple people can be print at a single time. Because of this, when you send a print request to a printer, it is assigned a job number. If you need to cancel your print job, this number will be used to remove the job from the print queue. Only the person who owns a print job can remove it from the queue, unless you happen to be the super user, or root.

 PostScript versus Non-PostScript   The assumption is made throughout this lesson that you will be printing to a PostScript printer. It is possible, however, that your system might be configured to interpret PostScript using a rasterizer and print to a non-PostScript printer.

The `line print` command (`lpr`) is the primary method for sending data to the printer. `lpr` essentially dumps data directly to the printer you specify. To use `lpr`, follow these steps:

1. Determine the name of the printer you want to use. This was probably set by your system administrator.

2. Choose the file you want to print. For the moment, only choose a text file. I'll discuss a few other formats shortly.

3. Send the print job by using **lpr -P*<printer name> <filename>* *<filename>* ....** If there is only one printer configured on your computer, chances are you can type **lpr *<filename>* *<filename>* ....**

For example

```
>lpr -PHOD samplefile.txt
```

The result of this command is that the file samplefile.txt is sent to the printer named HOD. (In case you're interested, HOD is my office printer, named the Heart of Darkness.) Depending on the load of the printer, the print job should be processed shortly.

 Printing More than One Copy   If you need to print multiple copies of a document, you don't need to send separate print jobs. Instead, you can specify the number of copies directly as an option to the `lpr` command. Follow `lpr` with **-#*<number of copies>*** to print that many copies of each file in the job.

There are a few file formats and special print cases that might require special attention from the `print` command. This special attention comes in the form of *filters* that are applied to the file and convert the information into a format that your printer can handle.

- **PS**—PostScript files. PostScript files should be handled automatically by the `lpr` command. You can print them as you would print a plain text file.

- **DVI**—TeX files. Files from TeX contain special page layout instructions. You can use the -d option with lpr in order to print these files correctly.

- **TR**—Troff files. This is the standard file format for man pages. If you'd like to print out a man page, you can use the -t option.

- **Text files with really long lines**—If you are having problems printing text files and having lines run off the end of the page, you can have the files reformatted on-the-fly so that they fit. To do this, use -p with lpr.

CHECKING THE STATUS OF A PRINT JOB: lpq

After you've sent a job to the printer, chances are you'll want to be able to check to see if it is done printing—especially if it is a network printer located on another floor in your building...or in another building altogether! To check the status of a job, you'll want to look at the queue for the printer that you submitted the job to. You do this with the **lpq -P<printer name>** command. Once again, if there is only a single printer on your system, you can issue lpq by itself.

For example

```
>lpq -PHOD

Rank    Owner     Job   Files              Total Size
1st     agroves   27    test.txt           19 bytes
2nd     jray      28    samplefile.txt     10021 bytes
```

This example shows that there are currently two different jobs in the printer queue for HOD. One is owned by agroves, and one is owned by jray. Each job is *ranked*, which shows the order in which it will print. The names of the files being printed are also shown, as well as the size and job ID number.

CANCELING A PRINT JOB: lprm

At times you might find that you've sent a print request to the printer, but didn't actually mean to—perhaps you sent a 3,000 page encyclopedia file instead of the three page report you intended. Whatever the case, the `lprm` command lets you remove items from the printer queue.

If you need to use `lprm`, follow these steps:

1. Use the `lpq` command to find the job ID number that you want to remove.

2. Invoke `lprm` with the syntax **lprm -P*<printer name>* *<job ID>*.**

For example, if I want to remove my job (job #28) from the queue in the preceding example, I would type

```
>lprm -PHOD 28
```

To verify the results, use `lpq` to check the queue again:

```
>lpq -PHOD
Rank    Owner     Job   Files              Total Size
1st     agroves   27    test.txt           19 bytes
```

My job is no longer in the queue, and will not be printed! Don't worry if you happen to accidentally enter in someone else's print job ID; you can only cancel your own jobs.

 Canceling Your Jobs If you would like to remove all the pending print jobs that you have sent, you can use the - character in place of the job ID. This cancels anything that you've sent to the printer.

PRETTY PRINTING: enscript

If you'd like to do some fancy printing, you can use the `enscript` command to convert your text files into PostScript, and add some flashy features. For instance, if you'd like to print two pages of text on a single side of paper, enscript can format your document correctly. It can also print banner information with each page to help you identify which file has been printed and which page number you are looking at. If your Linux distribution does not include enscript, check with one of the hundreds of Linux software sites, and you're sure to find a copy. An excellent starting point is http://www.linux.org.

To use enscript in its most basic form, do the following:

1. Choose your printer.

2. Choose the file that you want to print.

3. Run enscript like this: **enscript -d *<printer name>* *<filename>* *<filename>* ...**

For example, to use enscript to print my samplefile.txt file, I would do this:

```
>enscript -d HOD samplefile.txt
[ 1 pages * 1 copy ] sent to printer
```

Unlike lpr, enscript gives a bit of feedback on what is happening. Here it tells me that I've sent one page to the printer, and have requested the default number of copies: one. The output of this command, in its basic form, will be very similar to lpr. It simply dumps the file to the printer. The difference, however, is in command-line options that you can add to enscript to change the appearance of your printout. Here are a few of the options you can use:

- **Page range**—Use the option -a *<start page>*-*<end page>* to print a range of pages, rather than everything.

- **Pretty print source code**—If you're a programmer, enscript can print your source in an attractive format with highlights if you use the -E command-line switch.

- **Fancy header**—If you'd like to easily identify the file and page number that the text on a page belongs to, you can ask enscript to print a fancy header using -G.

- **Landscape mode**—Rather than printing across the short dimension of your page, the -r option will rotate the page 90 degrees and print in Landscape mode.

- **Multiple columns**—To print two pages of text per printed page, use the -2 option. You'll probably also want to use the -r Landscape mode switch so that everything fits appropriately.

- **Highlight bars**—If you're reading source code or spreadsheet-type data, you might find it difficult to follow a line across a page. Use the -H option to print light gray highlight bars across the page.

- **Multiple copies**—Using a slightly different syntax than lpr, enscript can print multiple copies of a job using the -n *<number of copies>* option.

Be sure to check the man pages for more information on enscript. There are many more options that you can use to further customize the appearance of your printouts.

SUMMARY

In this lesson, you learned the commands you need to print from the command line. If you're using an application in the KDE environment, it is actually using the same commands you've seen here to send information to the printer. The suite of lpr, lpq, and lprm commands make up the basis for printing from Linux and most UNIX computers. enscript is the icing on the cake. Let's review some of the highlights for this lesson:

- **lpr**—The lpr command is used to send a file to the printer. If the file is of a type other than plain text, it can be processed by filter to correctly format the information for your printer.

- **lpq**—When a print request is sent to the printer, either from lpr or enscript, it is added to the printer queue. Use the lpq function to display all pending printer transactions, their corresponding job IDs, and their owners.

- **lprm**—If you'd like to remove a job from the print queue, lprm will do the trick. You can use lprm to remove a single print job or all the jobs that you have pending at the printer.

- **enscript**—enscript is a useful utility for doing fancy printing on your printer. It allows multiple pages of text per printer page, pretty graphic headers, and a variety of other goodies.

LESSON 18

ACCESSING NETWORK RESOURCES

In this lesson you will learn about another strength of Linux—network connectivity.

You're now almost finished with your whirlwind tour of the Linux operating system, but nowhere near finished exploring and learning about the capabilities that Linux puts at your fingertips.

Linux excels at networking; with the proper configuration, you can spread Linux machines around the globe, and at each computer you log in, your user environment, files, and programs will all appear, just as they would at home.

With the same ease that your home environment can distribute itself to scattered machines to work for you, so can you distribute your workload to those same machines from your home machine. This lesson provides you with a survey of some of the programs that allow this distribution of workload.

telnet

`telnet` is a simple terminal program. In its primary use, it allows you to open a login session on a remote machine. To use the `telnet` command, issue the command as **telnet *<remote machine>***, where *<remote machine>* is either an IP address or a hostname. You should be prompted with a login and password prompt just as though you were sitting at the console of the remote machine.

telnet Particulars It's not unusual to run into situations where Backspace and Delete don't work properly at `telnet`'s login and password prompt. Don't be alarmed; this is simply an indication that the remote machine doesn't yet know what sort of terminal you're using. If the problem persists into the login session, see the section on `stty` in Lesson 16, "Modifying the User Environment."

rlogin

The `rlogin` command is very similar to the `telnet` command, except that it carries some user information along with the attempt to connect. If your account is good on several machines, they might be set up to allow you to connect between them without having to log in to each one. Try the `rlogin` command as **rlogin <remote machine>**. If you're lucky, you'll end up in a shell on the remote machine. If you're not, you'll be presented with a login prompt; from there, `rlogin` functions identically to `telnet`.

slogin

The `slogin` command is a remote terminal program that offers strong encryption of the data stream. If your machines have the secure-shell server running, you are strongly encouraged to use this command. Both the `rlogin` and `telnet` commands send your login and password information, as well as anything else you type, over the network in plain text. A malicious user with a small amount of easily available *cracker* software can *sniff* this information and compromise your account. (Please don't call them *hackers*. Hackers are quick and dirty, and often brilliant programmers—they don't break into things; crackers do.)

To find out whether the secure shell server is running, and to set up the `slogin` command (which needs quite a bit of configuration before you can use it) you are advised to contact your system administrator. He or she will be more than happy to tell you about the `slogin` command or any alternatives and to help you increase system security.

rn/trn

The rn and trn commands read Usenet newsgroups. Retreating slightly
into the background because of the World Wide Web, Usenet newsgroups
once were considered to be the collective memory of the Net. Even
though the Web has eclipsed newsgroups in terms of visibility, the fact
that newsgroups function as topic-oriented chat rooms and provide almost
real-time interaction makes them a useful source of help and information.
You can use the rn or trn command to access information that ranges
from the technical, to the idiotic, to the sublime. The rn and trn commands are executed by name, and internally take both single-key commands and multi-character commands followed by **<Return>**. The
following are the primary commands you need to know in rn or trn.

- **Listing Newsgroups**—l **<topic><Return>** will list all newsgroups that contain that topic. Keep your topics small parts of
  words—such as comp for computer topics—until you become
  familiar with the newsgroup naming conventions.

- **Going to a newsgroup**—g **<newsgroup name><Return>**, and
  then following the instructions.

- **For help**—h - no**<Return>**, will bring up rather copious
  context-sensitive help at almost any point in the program.

The trn command is a slightly more sophisticated version of rn, offering
article selection by subject thread, and you will probably prefer it if it's
available. Either version can be highly configured with command-line
switches and configuration files.

My trn Runs, but Doesn't Seem to Work? You prob-
ably don't have an NNTP (News) server configured.
Check Lesson 16 for an example on how to set the
NNTPSERVER environment variable.

ftp

The ftp command provides you with a way to retrieve files from remote
machines that aren't set up to share file systems with yours. If your

machine is running an FTP server, you might be able to use it to provide your files to the rest of the world as well. Contact your system administrator about this.

To use the ftp command, enter the command as ftp *<ftp server>*, where the FTP server is the IP address or hostname of a remote machine running an FTP server. If you've connected properly, you'll get a prompt for a username and password.

Some FTP servers allow you to connect without an account on the system. For these, use the username *anonymous*, and give your email address as the password.

After you're connected to an FTP site, you will be able to cd and ls your way around. Using the command **get** *<filename>* allows you to retrieve a file, and **put** *<filename>* allows you to send one from your directory to the remote system.

 Corrupting Your Data Some FTP servers will corrupt data unless you issue the binary command after you are connected. FTP servers actually try to fix the difference between the way that Linux and PC-type machines handle carriage returns in files, but they just end up messing things up when talking to another Linux machine. If you end up with corrupted files after you've downloaded them, try again, but issue the binary command before the get command.

WINDOWS CONNECTIVITY: smbclient, smbmount

If you are comfortable using ftp, and you happen to have to deal with a Windows-based network, you'll want to look into the smbclient command. smbclient allows you to connect to a Windows NetBIOS share as if it were an FTP site. You can use the same cd, ls, get, and put commands to navigate and interact with the file system. Unfortunately, you can only send and retrieve files from the shared resource—you cannot interact with files directly on the server. In order to do this, you'll need to have the Super User setup smbmount to mount the Windows share as a local drive. Whatever your Windows needs, however, Linux is ready to provide connectivity.

WEB BROWSERS: NETSCAPE, LYNX, AND KDE

You have a variety of browsers to use for accessing the World Wide Web. Let's take a look at a few.

NETSCAPE

Netscape is the GUI-based Web browser that is available on the largest number of Linux platforms. It functions in much the same way as the Macintosh or PC versions you might be familiar with already—point, click, repeat as necessary. If it's available on your system, you should be able to start Netscape by typing netscape from an X Windows terminal.

LYNX

Lynx is a text-based Web browser for those times when you're stuck in a text window; start it with **lynx <URL>**, and you will get a textual representation of the page that the URL points to. Lynx is a surprisingly full-featured browser for what you might think is an extremely limited market. The market is actually a bit bigger than you might think. Lynx starts and loads pages much faster than graphical-based browsers. This makes it a convenient alternative if you need to check some Web page quickly and don't need either the graphics or the wait.

KDE

Each file manager window in the KDE environment is also a full-function Web browser. Rather than starting a heavyweight program such as Netscape, you can type your destination URL into the URL line at the top of any file manager window, and you'll quickly be taken to the appropriate Web site.

EMAIL

Of all the network tools you'll make use of from your Linux account, email is likely to be the most frequently used. Email lets you communicate with your friends and colleagues, exchange files, and contact people all over the planet. As is fitting in its position as most used tool, email also has the widest range of software available. Most versions of Linux come with at least two different programs for accessing email, and frequently have a handful of others that have been installed over time. The following are some of the more commonly used programs for accessing and working with email:

- **mail**—Found on almost all Linux systems, mail is a command-line driven mail reading system. It's a fairly simple program without many customization features, but it's fast, and convenient to use if you don't need fancy mail filters or a menu-driven interface.

- **pine and elm**—These are both full-screen mail reading programs with simple and intuitive menus and configuration options. The pine program is somewhat more powerful than elm, but both are good mail readers for users who want convenience in a text-based email reader.

- **mh**—The Mail Handler. The mh suite of programs must be close to if not the least intuitive mail-reading package available. It is also, by far, the most powerful. The mh philosophy is very similar to the Linux philosophy—break the job at hand down into the smallest building blocks possible, make each of these programs, and let the user put them together to make any custom configuration desired. Only choose mh as your mail reader after you've become comfortable doing a bit of shell script programming, because you'll have to construct custom aliases and scripts before mh will show you its true power.

- **procmail**—The Mail Processor. The procmail program is designed to do sophisticated automatic processing of your email as it is received. If you would like to add automatic processing of your email to your account, you might want to check whether procmail is available on your system.

- **Graphical email interfaces**—Many desktop environments provide graphical email readers; for the user interested in the ultimate in point-and-click convenience, look to your desktop environment software. Netscape also provides an email client on Linux platforms, but it is only a POP mail client, and cannot read from your Linux mail spool unless your machine is also running a POP3 server. An example of the KDE email client (appropriately named Mail client) is shown in Figure 18.1.

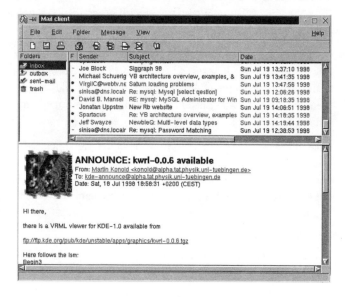

Figure 18.1   The KDE environment provides several graphical network clients, including an email client.

THE .FORWARD FILE

If you want email that comes to your account to automatically send itself somewhere else, you can make use of the .forward file. Not only can the .forward file be used to forward your email to another email address, but it can also be used to forward your email into programs, if you want to use software to process your email.

The format of the .forward file is simple:

> To forward your email to another email address, create a file named
> .forward in your home directory. In this file, put a single line con-
> taining the address to which you'd like your mail forwarded.
> Execute the command **chmod 644 ~/.forward** to set the permis-
> sions properly and you're finished. All email coming to your
> account will be forwarded to the new address.
>
> To forward your email into a program for automatic processing,
> create the .forward file in your home directory. In the .forward file,
> put a single line containing the pipe character ¦ followed by the
> path to the program you want to use. Run chmod on the file as in the
> preceding example, and you're done. Incoming email will be piped
> into whatever command you put in the .forward file.

SUMMARY

In this lesson, you were introduced to a sampling of tools that let you
make use of the network resources around you and around the world. As
you explore Linux, you'll find that this was really only a small sampling,
and that there are new tools for you to use appearing constantly. Some
will be replacements or upgrades for the commands outlined here, others
will be completely new. Don't be afraid to try them out. Here's a quick
review of this lesson's key points:

- **telnet**—Connects you to remote machines; if you have different
  accounts on different machines, you'll probably find yourself
  using it frequently.

- **rlogin**—Also connects you to remote machines, but is more
  useful than telnet if the machines you work on are configured
  to allow you to rlogin between them without giving a username
  or password.

- **slogin**—Provides security for remote connections. If you have
  it, use it. The network is becoming a very scary place with people breaking into Linux machines daily. Using the secure connection provided by slogin will protect your network traffic
  from prying eyes.

- **trn and rn**—Read Usenet newsgroups. Newsgroups can be a lot of fun and useful for finding information, but also can be a big drain on your time.

- **ftp**—Connects you with FTP servers and lets you transfer files around the world.

- **smbclient and smbmount**—Allow you to interact with Windows-based file sharing services.

- **Netscape is available for the Linux platform**—Lynx is a fast text-based Web browser. Both are useful for accessing Web resources. If you have KDE installed, it provides powerful built-in browsing features.

- **You're likely to have a wide choice of options for accessing email**—Check with other users of your system to find out what's available, and what local configuration information you need.

LESSON 19

PERMISSIONS

In this lesson, you will learn what permissions are, and how to change them.

Linux file permissions might be something that you never have to deal with. But, if your system has multiple users and you want to share files with them, chances are you'll need to know a bit about the concept of permissions and how to modify them.

OWNERS, GROUPS, AND PERMISSIONS

The owner of a file is exactly what it sounds like—the person who owns the file. Each file has information stored with it that identifies the account that owns it. Files can be *given* to other users by changing the owner information to match their username. In general, the person who creates a file is the person who owns it.

Each file on the Linux system also has a secondary piece of information stored that records the *group* ownership of the file. Groups are collections of users. By allowing a group to share ownership of files, multiple people can work together on a project and have their changes immediately available to other members of the group. By default, many Linux machine users each have their own group that is the same as their account name. This is a function of the utility that creates user accounts. In this case, when a user creates a file, the default group is that user's personal group. This is not necessarily the case on more traditional UNIX systems. The idea behind Linux machine users having personal groups is that creating a *users* group to encompass all the user accounts is a security risk.

Permissions control what actions a user can perform on a file or directory. There are three basic actions, which are pretty much self-explanatory: *read*, *write*, and *execute*. Read permissions control whether or not someone can view a file. Write allows or disallows changes to be made to a file. Execute permissions control whether or not a file can be run, or executed. In the case of a directory, these change a bit. If a directory has execute permissions turned off, you cannot cd into the directory, view its contents, or write to it. It is effectively turned off. If read permissions are turned off, you can still create files in the directory and read them, but you cannot get a listing of what is in the directory. Lastly, if the write permission is turned off for a directory, you can view a listing of the contents and read files, but not create any new files.

When permissions are applied to a file or folder, they are applied at three distinct levels: *owner*, *group*, and *world*. The owner permissions control what permissions the file owner has. Group permissions determine what actions can be performed by members of the same group that the file belongs to. Your system administrator can create new groups, or add you to be a member of a group. You can think of world permissions as being permissions for a huge group that encompasses *all* the users on your computer. If there is any sort of guest access to your computer, you can assume that any active world permissions apply to *anyone* who can access your computer.

CHECKING THE OWNER, GROUP, AND ASSOCIATED PERMISSIONS: `ls -lg`

You've already used the `ls` command extensively, but you probably haven't been paying too much attention to the extended information it can return. If you run `ls -lg` to list your directories, you can see the owner, group, and associated permissions for any file.

For example

```
>ls -lg
```

```
-rw-r--r--  1 jray   jray      2024 Oct 26 20:39 kiwi.tar
-rw-------  1 jray   test 1463882 Jul  2 11:33
➥magical-beans.gz
drwxrwxr-x  5 jray   test      1024 Nov  5 12:25 kyitn
...
```

The information you're interested in here are the first, third, and fourth columns:

- The first column identifies the owner, group, and world permissions that are active for a file or directory. The first character will be a d if the file type is a directory. Normally this will be an - for a normal file. The remainder of the characters, as you might guess, stand for read, write, and execute (x). The first three characters (following the initial - or d character) are the active owner permissions, the second three characters are the group permissions, and the last three are world permissions.

- The third column is the file owner.

- The fourth column is the group owner.

In this example, the kiwi.tar file has read/write permissions for the owner, and read permissions active for the group and world. The owner of the file is jray and the group the file belongs to is jray. The second file, magical-beans.gz, only has read/write permissions for the owner, who is jray. The group that magical-beans.gz belongs to is test, which has no permissions to operate on the file. The last file, kyitn is actually a directory. The owner of kyitn is jray, and the corresponding group is test. The owner and group both have full read, write, and execute permissions for this directory, whereas the world has read and execute.

CHANGING PERMISSIONS: chmod

Now that you know what permissions are, you'd probably like to know how to change them! This is accomplished with the chmod command. There are two modes of operation that you can use with chmod: a quick-and-dirty mode and a more user-friendly method of setting permissions.

The symbolic user-friendly mode uses easy-to-remember commands to set or unset permissions. To use this, do the following:

1. Pick a permission level. If you want to set permissions for the owner, this will be u. If you'd like to change permissions for the group, it is g. For world permissions, choose o. Lastly, if you'd like to affect all the levels of permissions (owner, group, and world), use a.

2. Choose an operation. Decide whether you want to set (turn on) or unset (turn off) a particular level of permission. If you want to set a permission, the operation will be +; if you want to unset a permission, it is -.

3. Choose the permission itself. If you'd like to operate on the read permission, this will be r; for write it is w, and for execute it is x.

4. Issue the chmod command in this manner:

   ```
   chmod <permission level><operation><permission>
   <filename> <filename> ....
   ```

For example, I want to activate group write permissions for the magical-beans.gz file shown earlier:

```
-rw------- 1 jray test   1463882 Jul  2 11:33
↪magical-beans.gz
```

```
>chmod g+w magical-beans.gz
```

To see if this worked, I'll run ls -lg on the filename.

```
>ls -lg magical-beans.gz
```

```
-rw--w---- 1 jray test   1463882 Jul  2 11:33
↪magical-beans.gz
```

Sure enough, write permissions are now active for the test group members.

Although this method for adjusting file permissions might be easy for some because of its symbolic nature, there is another syntax that I find faster and easier. This deals with setting the actual bit mask that controls a file's permissions. Turning on one of three binary bits can represent each level of permissions. The first of these bits (from right to left) controls read, the second controls write, and the third toggles execute.

Look at it this way:

```
100 - Read permission - The decimal equivalent of this
↪binary value is 4.
010 - Write permission - The decimal value for write is 2.
001 - Execute permission - The decimal representation is 1.
```

Using this technique, you can easily set multiple permissions at once. For example, it's easy to see that 110 is the combination of the read and write permissions. The decimal value of this binary string is 6 (4+2). To use this method of setting a file's permissions, you will set permissions for owner, group, and world simultaneously—with three digits. Each of these digits is the sum of the permissions that you'd like to set. The first digit is the owner, the second is the group, and the third is world.

For example, suppose I want to set the owner to have full permissions, and the group and world to have read and execute permissions. Full permissions are achieved by adding all the permission values 4+2+1=7. Read and execute permissions are a combination of 4+1=5. So the three numbers I'll use to set this are 7, 5, and 5, entered as a single three digit number, 755. The syntax for this form of chmod is **chmod <permissions> <filename> <filename> ....**

For example

```
>chmod 755 magical-beans.gz
>ls -lg magical-beans.gz

-rwxr-xr-x   1 jray test   1463882 Jul  2 11:33
➥magical-beans.gz
```

As I hoped, the owner has full read, write, and execute permissions, while the group and world have read and execute permissions. As you become experienced with permissions, you'll probably find that this second method is the fastest way to set permissions. Just remember read (4), write (2), and execute (1), and you'll be fine.

 Changing Permissions at the Directory Level   If you want to change the permissions of an entire directory structure (all the files and directories within a directory), you can use the command-line option -R with the chmod command to recursively change everything within a directory.

CHANGING A FILE'S OWNER: chown

This command isn't going to do you much good because it can only be
used by the super user (root). If you need to change the owner of a file,
you should ask your system administrator to run this for you. The syntax
for chown is **chown <new owner> <filename> <filename> ....**

For example

```
>chown agroves magical-beans.gz
>ls -lg magical-beans.gz

-rwxr-xr-x   1 agroves   test       1463882 Jul  2 11:33
➥ magical-beans.gz
```

The file is now owned by the user agroves as opposed to jray, who has
owned it throughout this lesson.

 Another Way to Grant Ownership If, for some reason, another user needs to own a file that you own,
you can always give them read permission and let
them copy the file. The copy that is created will be
owned by the other user.

CHANGING A FILE'S GROUP: chgrp

Although you can't change a file's owner, you can change the group that a
file belongs to with the chgrp command. To do this, however, you must be
a member of that group. Your system administrator has the ability to create new groups and add users to these groups. If you have any questions
about your own group membership(s), ask your administrator how your
account was configured.

To use chgrp, follow these steps:

1. Choose the file or files you want to change.

2. Determine the group that the file will now belong to.

3. Change the file's group using **chgrp <new group> <filename>
   <filename> ....**

For example

```
>chgrp admins magical-beans.gz
>ls -lg magical-beans.gz

-rwxr-xr-x   1 agroves   admins     1463882 Jul  2 11:33
➥magical-beans.gz
```

The magical-beans.gz file now belongs to the group admins. Members of the group have read and execute permissions for the file.

The most obvious use for chgrp is if you are collaborating on a project. If you create a file that you want to share with other people, you'll need to change the group of the file to be one that all the users belong to.

 Running chgrp on a Directory   The chgrp command, like chown, can also be run recursively on a directory by using the -R option. This is a big time saver when you want to modify a bunch of files and directories at a time.

LOGGING IN TO A NEW GROUP: newgrp

If you're working on a project, you might not want to constantly change the group of the files that you create; this would get pretty monotonous if you are working with hundreds of files. Luckily, there is a way to log in to a group that you are a member of. This is done by way of the newgrp command. All files that are created after executing this command will be under the group membership that you've switched to. This change will persist until you log out or use the newgrp command again. Use newgrp by typing **newgrp <new group>**.

For example

```
>newgrp admins
```

After this command is executed, all further files that are created in this session will belong to the group admins.

BECOMING ANOTHER USER TEMPORARILY: su

The substitute user command, su, lets you switch to another user account from within a single login session. Under Linux, this changes your *effective* user ID—which means that all files created will effectively be as if the other user created them. Your *actual* user ID remains the same, however. A noticeable side effect of this is that even though you've used su to become another user, running mail will check email for the user account you initially used to log in. To use the su command, enter it as **su <user to switch to>**.

For example

```
>su agroves

Password: ******
```

I can now use the whoami command to verify that the system now believes that I am effectively agroves.

```
>whoami

agroves
```

Just as I suspected! I can perform operations under the agroves account. If you think that you can use su to try to guess other users' passwords, guess again! The su command logs all accesses to a system log file.

 Account Sharing Guidance   It isn't a good idea to share account passwords between users. For this example, I've used the agroves account, which isn't necessarily good. Because the system thinks I'm agroves, most anything I do will be logged as being done by that user...and she might not appreciate it very much.

A more proper use of su would be to switch to non-personal accounts. There are several accounts that are owned by database servers, and so on, which would be prime candidates for the appropriate use of su in order to perform maintenance on the database files.

SUMMARY

In this lesson, you learned the purpose of permissions, owners, and groups. You should now understand what is necessary to enable other users to access your files and how to collaborate on projects using group permissions. You might want to take a few minutes to talk to your system administrator to find out how he or she has decided to manage groups. Also, you might want to request that groups be created which include other users that you will want to share files with. Let's take a look at some of the highlights from this lesson:

- **Permissions**—File permissions control who can access a file and what level of access they have to a file. The three levels of permissions are read, write, and execute. These permissions can be applied to the owner, group, or world.

- **chmod**—The chmod command changes the permissions for a file or directory. There are two methods of operation—symbolic and numeric. They both accomplish the same thing, use whichever you feel comfortable with.

- **chown**—Only the super user can change who owns a file. If you can convince your administrator to do so, chown will change the owner.

- **chgrp**—You can change the group that a file belongs to with the chgrp command. You can only change the file to a group that you belong to.

- **newgrp**—Rather than constantly having to change the group for files you create, you can use newgrp to log in to a group that you are a member of. All files that are created for the remainder of your login session will be created under that group.

- **su**—The substitute user command effectively switches to another user within a single login session. If you have the password of another account, you can use su to perform operations under this account; any files you create will be owned by this user.

LESSON 20

PRIVILEGED COMMANDS

In this lesson, you'll take a look at some of the special commands Linux users seldom encounter.

The commands in this lesson are restricted to being run by the root user, but the information here will help you understand some of root's concerns and help conversations with your system administrator to make a little more sense.

Because of the way that Linux works (with multiple users, multiple processes, and files owned by potentially hundreds of people), there are certain commands that would cause chaos if entrusted to normal users. These commands do things such as format disks, reboot the system, and create or remove devices.

SINGLE-USER MODE

Every Linux machine can be configured to boot into Single-User mode—a mode where the machine has no network resources, and can only support a single user logged in. This mode is a maintenance mode that allows the root user to repair problems with the system without having to worry about other users changing things that they are working on. With some versions of Linux, if a machine experiences a particularly hard crash, it might reboot itself into Single-User mode automatically. Some require a root password before any commands can be entered, but others come up directly into a root shell. If you happen to crash a Linux machine and it comes up into Single-User mode, *Do Not Touch Anything!* Anything you do has the potential to make diagnosing the crash impossible, and worse, could have devastating effects on the system. For the root user, a single-keystroke typo in the `rm` command can delete the entire file system, from the top down.

fsck

Every now and then you might hear a system administrator grumbling about having to fsck a drive. Linux tends to take reasonably good care of its drives, but problems do occasionally crop up. The fsck command is Linux's disk fixer program, which is used to clean up problems caused by crashes or errant pieces of software. Most Linux systems fsck their drives on startup, and the expected result is an analysis report containing the number of files and the fragmentation level of the drive. If you're watching a Linux machine boot, do not be overly concerned if you see fsck report problems—Linux will automatically attempt to fix them. In most cases it will be successful, and after fscking the drives the system will restart the reboot process. If the drives have serious problems, the automatic fsck will exit with an error message stating Run fsck manually. If it does, don't touch anything. Go find a system administrator.

mount/umount

The mount command tells the system to attach a disk drive to the file system at a particular directory. If you remember from Lesson 4, "The File System," Linux abstracts the physical hardware by causing drives to appear as directories in the file system. The mount command tells the system how to access the drive or where to locate it on the network, and where to attach it to the file system. The umount command does exactly the opposite—it removes mounted devices.

If you log in to the system and are greeted by a message that says something such as No Home Directory - using / don't panic. In all likelihood your home directory is fine, it's just on a drive that is not mounted. This shouldn't happen often, but with drives and resources being shared over the network, it only takes one person tripping over a network patch cable to make some devices unavailable until the wire can be repaired.

If you get the preceding error, or on some systems, you are kicked right back off the system after entering your password, wait 15 minutes and try again before calling your system administrator. Chances are, they already know about the problem and are trying to fix it, but dozens of users calling to complain is slowing them down.

shutdown/reboot

While personal computers are becoming increasingly picky about being shut down instead of simply turned off, Linux machines are more picky still. The difference, of course, goes back to the fact that Linux uses dozens of cooperating programs to form what appears as the operating system. Each of these programs could be in the process of modifying, moving, creating, or deleting files at any point in time. If you simply shut off the power to a Linux machine, you interrupt all these processes, and probably destroy any files they were working on at the time. If the files were things such as word-processor documents, this would be only a minor problem. Unfortunately, Linux also moves around and updates files critical for the operating system. Simply shutting off the power to a Linux machine has the potential to completely corrupt the drives, leaving the system unusable—in short, don't do it.

To prevent this problem, Linux has a shutdown command and a reboot command, each with obvious goals. These two commands gracefully exit all running software, write out disk-cache information to the drives, and complete their respective tasks. They are restricted to the root user for obvious reasons, yet Linux allows the console user to press **Ctrl+Alt+Del**. This doesn't actually turn the machine off; it executes the shutdown command, as root, without requiring a password. Only use this in extreme emergencies. Other users could be using your machine, or your machine could be providing disk resources to other machines. Shutting it down is likely to create havoc on your local network and will earn you a high position on your system administrator's list of least favorite users.

chown

The chown command is used to change the owner of a file from one account to another. Obviously, a normal user can't use this command, but if you need this done, your system administrator can do it for you. Remember, you can always get a copy of a file that you can read by using the cp command—changing ownership might not be necessary.

SUMMARY

In this lesson, you were introduced to a few things that you shouldn't or can't do in the hopes that understanding why you shouldn't and can't do them will make interaction with your system administrator easier. System administrators have a hard job; they have to walk the fine line between keeping the system functioning for all users (which sometimes requires them to be hard-nosed and inflexible) and creating the environment the individual users need to work. Most are truly interested in making the system work the best it possibly can for you, but many do not have sufficient time to have a lot of patience. Hopefully, an understanding of the types of things that will make your system administrator's life more difficult, and why it is you shouldn't do them, will allow you to stay on the good side of your administrator. Now, let's review some of the other points from this lesson:

- Never touch a machine if it looks like its running a root shell.

- Don't bother root (your system administrator) about unmounted drives unless it's obvious that nobody knows about it.

- Never ever turn the power to your machine off without permission from your administrator.

- Root (administrative users) can change ownership of files for you, but you should consider whether it's really necessary, or whether a copy will do.

APPENDIX A

SELECTING YOUR LINUX DISTRIBUTION

Before you can even install Linux and start using it, you need to make a choice that can be a bit confusing: What distribution of Linux should you use? If you were to do a search for Linux Distribution on the Internet, you'll find references to Red Hat, Caldera, Debian, and many, many others. With the growing popularity of Linux among users and developers, this list will undoubtedly continue to grow in the upcoming months and years.

Selecting the one that is right for you is bound to be difficult if you have no experience with Linux. Luckily, most of the distributions are available for free or for a minimal cost on CD-ROM, so you have the opportunity of testing a few without spending thousands of dollars. Most people find a distribution and stick with it religiously. Others patch together a hybrid system using pieces of many distributions. It's your operating system; it's up to you.

 What Is a Linux Distribution? A Linux distribution is nothing more than a *packaging* of the Linux operating system. Just as car dealers add options to a base model car, the people who create the different Linux distributions add features to their version to make it appealing.

KEY POINTS TO CONSIDER

Version—Does the distribution include the most recent stable version of the Linux kernel? (As of this writing, 2.0.36 is the most current distributed kernel, with 2.2.0 on the horizon.) The *kernel* contains the basic instructions that Linux needs to operate. Low-level system problems, such as susceptibility to TCP/IP network attacks, are often kernel-level problems. New versions of the kernel are released over time, which patch any problems that are found. If you select a distribution that *isn't* up to date, you might find yourself needing to upgrade the kernel manually—which can be a tricky undertaking for a new user.

Ease of Upgrading—In the past, upgrading Linux has been a matter of checking to see if a new version of the software is available, downloading it, compiling the program, and installing it. This leads to outdated files lingering in hidden directories on the system, lost configuration files, and, in general, headaches. Many Linux distributions now include the capability to analyze your system and determine what files need to be upgraded, and then perform the upgrade automatically. This keeps you up to date with the latest patches and utilities and reduces the amount of time you must spend administrating the machine.

Included Features—At the base of any Linux distribution, you'll find all the standard utilities and goodies you expect. In fact, in most cases if something isn't included, there's no reason why you can't locate it on the Internet, and then install it on your system. This can be a bit inconvenient if you're dealing with hundreds of machines, however. Pick the distribution that has the most features that appeal to you. You can add what you need later, but its best to start out with a solid foundation.

Support—This, for many, might be the most important thing to think about. If you purchase a full Linux distribution, do you get support for the software? The capability to get quick technical information and help from a single contact point can be very important for businesses and individuals alike. Rather than choosing a product that leaves you to your own resources, you might want to pick one that includes support.

A FEW POPULAR DISTRIBUTIONS

At this point, I'm going to quickly look at a few popular Linux distributions and give a brief overview of some of their features. A distribution can change drastically from one version to another, so you'll probably want to research them a bit on your own to find out what is or isn't included in the most current distribution—which might very well be different from what is available at the time I am writing this.

A Few Points of Caution

- Most Linux distributions that you can purchase for $50+ are also available for free over the Internet or on cheaply priced CD-ROMs. Although these versions are similar, the cheap versions *do not* include any sort of support, printed documentation, or normally included commercial software. You are entirely on your own. If you want a complete product, make sure you're buying a boxed package.

- Linux distributions have their own versioning scheme. For example, Red Hat is currently at version 5.2, while Caldera OpenLinux is 1.3. Both of these products, however, are using the Linux kernel 2.0.35. Just because one distribution's version number is lower than another doesn't mean that it is older or less capable. To be sure, compare kernel versions, which are usually listed on the box.

RED HAT LINUX

Red Hat is the most popular version of Linux in the United States and includes a variety of value-added packages. The installation process is streamlined, and can be performed over a network very easily. Many custom utilities are included for managing the system graphically. Red Hat also pioneered, and includes, the RPM packaging system that makes upgrading between different distribution versions as easy as clicking an *upgrade* button and waiting a few minutes. Red Hat also provides support services for the full version of their products.

For more information on the Red Hat distribution, look at http://www.redhat.com.

DEBIAN LINUX

The Debian Linux distribution is also a very popular, non-commercial distribution of Linux. Support is provided through the Debian development community, which consists of hundreds of people worldwide. The Debian distribution is a cutting-edge distribution that is updated on a very frequent basis. Bugs are tracked and patched as quickly, if not quicker, than many commercial distributions. Debian also provides their own package management system, which, similar to RPM, handles upgrades in a very seamless and fashion. Debian Linux is the most flexible of the distributions, but this flexibility means that new users will experience a great deal of added complexity. Debian Linux is thus best used by Linux or UNIX veterans.

For more information on Debian, try http://www.debian.org.

CALDERA OPENLINUX

The Caldera commercial Linux distribution is a commercial power-user distribution that includes several high-end servers, including the new Linux Sybase ASE (SQL) Server. Caldera has built a user-friendly installation procedure that is similar to Red Hat's, also using the RPM package manager. A particularly nice feature of OpenLinux is that it comes with KDE, which provides a wonderful interface for users coming from more traditional desktop operating systems. It also provides the StarOffice productivity suite, which offers Office 95 connectivity and very similar functionality and features. For corporate customers, Caldera offers extensive training programs, certification, and support services for OpenLinux.

To learn more about Caldera OpenLinux, take a look at http://www.calderasystems.com.

S.u.S.E. Linux

This is a solid, full–featured distribution that comes with 4 CD-ROMs of applications and source code and very extensive printed documentation. The S.u.S.E. distribution uses the Red Hat RPM package management system for easy upgrades, and includes its own easy-to-use administration tools. It also comes with X Windows servers that have been developed by S.u.S.E. to support the latest video card offerings. For the graphically oriented, it also includes the KDE Desktop Environment.

For more information about S.u.S.E., go to `http://www.suse.com`.

So Many to Choose From...

Whatever distribution you choose, you're bound to find features that you like in it, but that aren't included in others. If you're making decisions for a company, you might want to test the level of responsiveness of the support services for several distributions. It's difficult to choose a clear winner because of the rapid pace of Linux development. If you're interested in further research of the different distributions, check out this page at the *Linux Headquarters* Web site: `http://www.linuxhq.com/dist-index.html`.

Luckily, the cost of commercial distributions of Linux is far less than competing mainstream operating systems. For the cost of one copy of a commercial UNIX or NT, you can own *many* distributions of Linux. Take time to find one that you like, and that includes the features and software you're likely to need. Exploring the options that Linux opens up to you is half the fun of running the operating system!

INDEX

SYMBOLS

A

Q-R

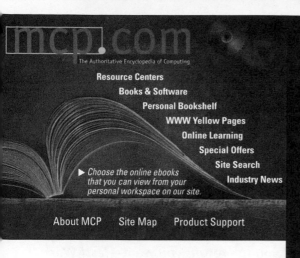

SAMS
Teach Yourself
in 10 Minutes

Quick steps for fast results™

Sams Teach Yourself in 10 Minutes *gets you the results you want—fast! Work through the 10-minute lessons and learn everything you need to know quickly and easily. It's the handiest resource for the information you're looking for.*

Sams Teach Yourself UNIX in 10 Minutes
William Ray
ISBN: 0-672-31523-8
$12.99 US/$18.95 CAN

Other Sams Teach Yourself in 10 Minutes Titles

PCs
Shelley O'Hara
ISBN: 0-672-31322-7
$12.99 US/$18.95 CAN

The Internet
Paul Cassel
ISBN: 0-672-31320-0
$12.99 US/$18.95 CAN

HTML 4
Tim Evans
0-672-31325-1
$12.99 USA/$18.95 CAN

PC Upgrades
Galen A. Grimes
ISBN: 0-672-31323-5
$12.99 US/$18.95 CAN

PalmPilot and Palm III
Michael Steinberg
0-672-31452-5
$12.99 USA/$18.95 CAN

All prices are subject to change.

SAMS

www.samspublishing.com